MW01296671

Angels, Giants, and Things under the Earth

Angels, Giants, and Things under the Earth

DARK STUDIES

Joseph Dulmage

Copyright © 2016 Joseph Dulmage
All rights reserved.

ISBN: 1532709064
ISBN 13: 9781532709067
Library of Congress Control Number: 2016906070
CreateSpace Independent Publishing Platform
North Charleston, South Carolina

To James, whose enthusiasm and curiosity encourages long, yet never tiring Bible study; ever proving God giveth understanding according to his words. Mining truth as gold, we have considered the days of old, the years of ancient times, and the future seems upon us.

Ecclesiastes 3:15 That which hath been is now; and that which is to be hath already been; and God requireth that which is past.

Introduction

§

THE BIBLE'S MESSAGE REGARDING MANKIND's spiritual relationship with God and our need for salvation constitutes scripture's constant primary purpose. Within its pages, men and women find an inexhaustible resource for help, encouragement, and instruction. No other book fills the hearts and minds of so many people.

The Bible also includes other topics, mysterious and thought provoking histories, some only briefly mentioned, yet they bequeath to readers a thirst for more understanding. Often these scriptures present dark truth. Inevitably, different opinions and ideas emerge around them; hence passionate dialogue commences among Christians. This book seeks to understand the provocative, less traveled biblical roads, an exploration of an age before God created man- as well as the days of Noah. The book concludes with the future, an age where many ancient developments come back around to haunt us yet again.

God is the same yesterday, today, and forever; his gifts and intentions remain unwaveringly steadfast. Antithetically, in darkest parallel, orchestraters of evil and rebellion remain stubbornly persistent. Angels, Giants, and Things under the Earth takes a serious look at the days of Noah, and the uncomfortable equivalences it has with our own times.

Contents

Introduction · vii

Days of Noah · 1
What's wrong with animals? · · · · · · · · · · · · · · · · · · · 6
Biological Creativity · 10
Giants Survive · 14
Giant Culture · 17
Degeneration · 20
Naming Angels · 25
One World Government · 30
Things under Earth · 34
Grapes and Blood · 43
King of Salem · 56
Introducing Melchizedek · 57
Salem · 59
Priest Melchizedek · 61
Melchizedek's Origin · 70
Examining the Curse · 72
GAP · 84
GAP · 86
Counting Backward · 88

Void · 90
The Deep · 93
Universal Flood · 96
Opposing Views · 98
Genesis Chapter 1 · 102
Light Years · 106
Replenish · 108
Angels · 111
Lucifer's Fall · 114
King of Tyrus · 117
Prince of Tyrus · 120
A Previous Age · 122
Music · 125
Cherub's Physical Appearance · · · · · · · · · · · · 128
The Serpent's Curse · 134
Serpent's Seed · 137
Man of Sin/Son of Perdition · · · · · · · · · · · · · 143
Mystery of Iniquity · 147
Daniel's Fourth Kingdom · · · · · · · · · · · · · · · · 151
The Last Superpower · 152
Gentile Kingdoms · 155
Historical Foundations · · · · · · · · · · · · · · · · · · 159
Second Return · 164
Jews Return Unconverted · · · · · · · · · · · · · · · · 166
Burdensome Stone · 170
Why Jerusalem Provokes War · · · · · · · · · · · · · 172
Antichrist and Jerusalem · · · · · · · · · · · · · · · · 174
Great Religious Leader · · · · · · · · · · · · · · · · · · 179
Three Babylons · 184
Mystery Babylon · 189
Fourth Kingdom Emerges · · · · · · · · · · · · · · · · 195

The End Game· 197
America and Babylon · 200
The Approaching Day · 211
The Bride and Daniel's 70th Week · · · · · · · · · · · · · · · 216
What is the falling away? · 223
Counting Days · 230
Jesus' Warning · 236
Salvation · 238

About the Author · 245
Glossary · 247

Days of Noah

§

THE TERM DAYS OF NOAH refers to the biblical age when people became so wicked that God judged the world with a flood and started over. Jesus actually referenced the era to explain how humanity lives shortly before his 2ⁿᵈ Advent; but mankind's advancing wickedness is only part of the story. Interpreting Jesus' prophecy literally infers the last days' likeness to the *days of Noah* -includes all areas of human experience. Did Jesus mean science and technology mirrors Noah's generation? What about the horrifying fact of fallen angels marrying human women and producing a race of giants. Did Jesus imply that happens again too?

Matthew 24:37 *But as the days of Noe were, so shall also the coming of the Son of man be.*

SONS OF GOD

Genesis 6:1-4 *And it came to pass, when men began to multiply on the face of the earth, and daughters were born unto them, 2 That the sons of God saw the daughters of men that they were fair; and they took them wives of all which they chose. 3 And the LORD said, My spirit shall not always strive with man, for that he also is flesh: yet his days shall be an hundred and twenty years. 4 There were giants in the earth in those days; and also* *after that, when the sons of God came in unto the daughters of men, and they bare children to them, the same became mighty men which were of old, men of renown.*

The context of these verses makes a distinction between *the sons of God* and the *daughters of men*. These distinctions reveal more than a moral or spiritual difference because the union produces a giant. These sons of God are male, but they are not human beings. The term *sons of God -is* again used to identify angels in Job. Using scripture with scripture the Bible interprets itself. Sons of God, in Genesis 6 and in Job, are angels. In the New Testament, God refers to Christians as sons of God, but the context is clear. For one to argue the sons of God in Genesis 6 are human beings is meritless.

Job 1:6-7 Now there was a day when the sons of God came to present themselves before the LORD, and Satan came also among them. 7 And the LORD said unto Satan, Whence comest thou? Then Satan answered the LORD, and said, From going to and fro in the earth, and from walking up and down in it.

Job 2:1-2 Again there was a day when the sons of God came to present themselves before the LORD, and Satan came also among them to present himself before the LORD. 2 And the LORD said unto Satan, From whence comest thou? And Satan answered the LORD, and said, From going to and fro in the earth, and from walking up and down in it.

Job 38:7 When the morning stars sang together, and all the sons of God shouted for joy?

Being male these angels produced a seed capable of fertilizing a woman's egg. This unholy copulation birthed a giant, a confused mixture of Adam's race and angelic stock. Unquestionably a horrifying development and a situation which deeply grieved God, but this is exactly what happened in the days of Noah. Not only were some angels genetically corrupting the seed of men, but human beings completely succumbed to the depravity of their carnal nature.

Genesis 6:5-6 And GOD saw that the wickedness of man was great in the earth, and that every imagination of the thoughts of his heart was only evil continually. 6 And it repented the LORD that he had made man on the earth, and it grieved him at his heart.

Some Bible students reject the interpretation angels took human women in marriage, largely based upon Jesus' statement angels are not given in marriage. Jesus corrected a particular group of Jewish leaders, the Sadducees, about the resurrection. In the course of his instruction the Lord references angels and marriage.

Matthew 22:29-30 Jesus answered and said unto them, Ye do err, not knowing the scriptures, nor the power of God. 30 For in the resurrection they neither marry, nor are given in marriage, but are as the angels of God in heaven.

Notice Jesus refers to good angels in heaven, while Genesis 6 deals with evil angels on earth. In the days of Noah, exceptional deviant angels rebelled and kept not their first estate, and left their own habitation. Furthermore, and most importantly, the marriages in Genesis 6 did not produce normal children; their offspring were giants!

Another argument against the sons of God being angels is the idea angels are asexual (neither male nor female). That theory, however, is biblically unfounded. Every time the Bible mentions an angel, he is always male. The Bible never mentions female or sexless angels.

New Testament Corroboration

In the New Testament, Peter and Jude present information concerning a unique group of evil angels. Notice the angels discussed are in the context of Noah's Flood.

2 Peter 2:4-5 For if God spared not the angels that sinned, but cast them down to hell, and delivered them into chains of darkness, to be reserved unto judgment; 5 And spared not the old world, but saved Noah the eighth person, a preacher of righteousness, bringing in the flood upon the world of the ungodly;

Jude 1:6-7 *And the angels which kept not their first estate, but left their own habitation, he hath reserved in everlasting chains under darkness unto the judgment of the great day. 7 Even as Sodom and Gomorrha, and the cities about them in like manner, giving themselves over to fornication, and going after strange flesh, are set forth for an example, suffering the vengeance of eternal fire.*

Peter and Jude discuss a group of angels whose behavior resulted in judgment and incarceration in hell. This is very interesting, because Satan and his angels are presently free to roam the first and second heavens. Satan and his angels receive judgment at the Great White Throne Judgment, which does not take place until after the Millennium. While these particular angels are in hell thousands of years ahead of schedule, the very angels defined as those who left their habitation and their first estate Therefore, logical thinking concludes theses angels are the sons of God who married human women. What other conclusion is even possible?

Notice the comparison *even as* in *Jude 1:7*, to Sodom and Gomorrah. All things in the physical world represent some kind of spiritual truth. God compared certain aspects of *Genesis 6* -to Sodom and Gomorrah. Going after strange flesh in *Genesis 6*- were male angels taking human women. In the days of Lot, strange flesh was human males with human males. It is important to realize Jude is not commenting on the whole societal condition, but rather one element. I mention this because many persons think of only one thing when they remember Sodom and Gomorrah. God gives a more complete assessment in the summary below. Sexual abomination seems to be their final disregarding of God.

Ezekiel 16:48-50 *As I live, saith the Lord GOD, Sodom thy sister hath not done, she nor her daughters, as thou hast done, thou and thy* *daughters.* **49 Behold, this was the iniquity of thy sister Sodom, pride, fulness of bread, and abundance of idleness was in her and in her daughters, neither did she strengthen the hand of the poor and needy. 50 And they were haughty, and committed abomination before me: therefore I took them away as I saw good.**

God comparing evil angels to Sodom and Gomorrah correlates the days of Noah to the last days; those being days close to Jesus' 2nd Advent. Thus a thorough understanding of the days of Noah and the days of Lot become critical in understanding the signs of the times in one's own country. Jesus' prophecy corresponds directly with *Ezekiel 16:48-50.*

Luke 17:26-30 And as it was in the days of Noe, so shall it be also in the days of the Son of man. 27 They did eat, they drank, they married wives, they were given in marriage, until the day that Noe entered into the ark, and the flood came, and destroyed them all. 28 Likewise also as it was in the days of Lot; they did eat, they drank, they bought, they sold, they planted, they builded; 29 But the same day that Lot went out of Sodom it rained fire and brimstone from heaven, and destroyed them all. 30 Even thus shall it be in the day when the Son of man is revealed.

Observe Jesus says people engage in many normal behaviors: eating, drinking, marrying, buying and selling, building, and farming. Activities not sinful in and of themselves, in fact, the apparent normalcy of things lull people into a slumbering, spiritual ignorance. Interpreting the passage alongside *Ezekiel 16:48-50* - however, brings full understanding. A nation's successful governing, results in much idleness or free time and plenty of food. Fewer and fewer people credit God for earthly benefits. People become arrogant and haughty; sexual behaviors become extreme and perverted.

Thought to ponder: The more successful a nation, sinful behaviors become more arrogant and proud.

What's wrong with animals?

§

JOB 12:7 BUT ASK NOW the beasts, and they shall teach thee; and the fowls of the air, and they shall tell thee:

But there is more wrong with this ancient world than human and angelic wickedness. God repents for having made animal life as well. As discriminating Bible students, we need to ask why God is sorry he made the animals.

Genesis 6:7 *And the LORD said, I will destroy man whom I have created from the face of the earth; both man, and beast, and the creeping thing, and the fowls of the air; for it repenteth me that I have made them.*

Consider animals and how they differ from men. Besides obvious differences like intellect and appearance, a basic moral inequality exists. Animals are not in rebellion against God; men are. Animals act purely on instinct. Of course, certain animals trained by men achieve some desired behaviors, but they act in submission to a higher will and not their own. In other words, animals do not sin. So why is God repenting about making the animals?

Apparently something happened to the animals in the days of Noah, something so terrible God declared their lives must end. Jesus made a prophetic statement, which if considered carefully, takes on huge implications and provides logical reasons for the near total destruction of animal life, preserving only selected animals on the ark.

Matthew 24:37 *But as the days of Noe were, so shall also the coming of the Son of man be.*

Again, what exactly does the above statement mean? What happened in the days of Noah? Nearly all Christians interpret this prophecy in a moral and spiritual context only; that is we tend to think about Noah's generation being morally reprehensible and totally degenerate. But then (and there) the thinking stops. We think very little about the sciences or the technology of Noah's world.

What kind of sciences and technology existed? A literal interpretation of Jesus' prophecy means Noah's generation looked a lot like it does today? Do you think the ancient world experimented with genetic research? Do you think they used electricity? What about computers? Why do people limit interpretation of *Matthew 24:37* -to moral and spiritual likeness? As I write in year 2002 AD, the 2nd Coming of Jesus Christ rapidly approaches. If you want to know what the days of Noah were like, look around. Our present world is morally wicked and very technologically advanced, just as the days of Noah.

Someone asks: If the antediluvians were truly advanced as we are today, why can't we find archeological evidence? Answer: Most of Noah's earth remains underwater, and it is easier to explore the surface of the moon than to explore depths greater than 3,000 feet. Furthermore, Noah's Flood was so horrendous it obliterated almost everything. The evidence of Noah's world is buried under miles of mud and then covered with 10,000 (or more) feet of water. When the flood waters abated, most the planet stayed under water inaccessible to exploration.

THE AGE OF GENETIC RESEARCH

Just as history identifies a previous time as the *industrial revolution*, and then more recently the *computer age*, the present era is being hailed as an *age of genetics*. Science has entered a new age of genetic possibilities. Where will this take us? Are human beings playing God? Things sounding like science fiction a few years ago reveal today's reality. Cloning, test tube babies, granting patents for new life forms- all this and more takes place today. Many people believe science is on the verge of eliminating birth defects, neurological disorders, even slowing down if not stopping the ageing process.

But genetic research also brings danger. In a rush to do something good for mankind, new viruses may emerge. Science tampering with genetic structure creates new life forms, possibly threatening people. Proposals to grow human beings with only brain stems (no higher brain) are actually being considered; like plants a people crop cultivated to provide organs and body parts for transplants. Biological defects detected early in fetus development results in children aborted on the spot. Sound like a fantasy nightmare? Listen closely to your nightly news.

Quite possibly, in the days of Noah, science engaged in genetic experimentation with animals, and something went wrong. The sons of God, intervening with human science, corrupted God's creation. God took drastic measures to ensure a pure, uninfected human and animal life survived by segregating and preserving them on Noah's ark. God says all flesh is corrupt, not just human. Notice also God blames a mysterious group referred to as *them* for the problems. The *them* are the fallen angels.

*Genesis 6:11-14 The earth also was corrupt before God, and the earth was filled with violence. 12 And God looked upon the earth, and, behold, it was corrupt; for **all flesh had corrupted his way upon the earth**. 13 And God said unto Noah, The end of all flesh is come before me; for **the earth is filled with violence through them**; and, behold, I will destroy them with the earth. 14 Make thee an ark of gopher wood; rooms shalt thou make in the ark, and shalt pitch it within and without with pitch.*

The passage below associates the word *perfect* with the word *generation*. The word *generation* deals with Noah's genetic purity. Thus the word generation, in this case, is dealing with genes and/or genetic structure. In other words, God preserved only genetically unaltered animals on the ark.

*Genesis 6:8-9 **But** Noah found grace in the eyes of the LORD. **9** These are the generations of Noah: Noah was a just man and perfect in his generations, and Noah walked with God.*

THOUGHT TO PONDER:

Dinosaurs may be linked to the days of Noah. On a timeline, this conflicts with carbon dating, but science does not acknowledge an earth completely under water. The enormous pressures from this catastrophic event are not considered in dating examination. Furthermore, theory launched from the supposed fact of evolution, produces effectually skewed conclusions. If one's premise is considered fact, when in reality it is not fact, resulting conclusions need reconsidered.

Biological Creativity

§

BESTIALITY OR SOMETHING ELSE?

GOD LABELS BESTIALITY CONFUSION. WHEN persons committed such gross offense against nature the beast and its seducer received a death sentence; such behavior with an animal ruins the creature's spirit.

Leviticus 18:23 Neither shalt thou lie with any beast to defile thyself therewith: neither shall any woman stand before a beast to lie down thereto: it is confusion.

Leviticus 20:15-16 And if a man lie with a beast, he shall surely be put to death: and ye shall slay the beast. 16 And if a woman approach unto any beast, and lie down thereto, thou shalt kill the woman, and the beast: they shall surely be put to death; their blood shall be upon them.

Under laboratory conditions, conception is possible between man and beast. A little genetic tampering with sperm and egg procreates unbelievable evil. It happened in the past and it happens in the future. In the days of Noah, bestiality was not practiced solely for debased sexual gratification. An already highly advanced society with the help of supernatural intellect carried out genetic experiments. Satan's goals were to procreate animal life forms (in rebellion against God) with the biological capacity to reproduce.

If this is all sounding a bit much, let the reader examine *Revelation chapter 9* with utmost scrutiny. Notice John describes two specific armies. These creatures are not the armies of the Chinese, nor are they the attempted description of modern weaponry by Apostle John. These things are genetically confused organisms, which compose devil armies' right from the pit of hell. And if that were not enough, these devils are led by angels.

Army #1 is led by an angel named Apollyon, king of the bottomless pit. The demonic hosts are confused organisms containing body parts from the following: locusts, horses, men, women, lions, and scorpions. Read carefully these creatures' description. How do you suppose they got in this condition? Do you think God created them this way?

Revelation 9:2-3 And he opened the bottomless pit; and there arose a smoke out of the pit, as the smoke of a great furnace; and the sun and the air were darkened by reason of the smoke of the pit. 3 And there came out of the smoke locusts upon the earth: and unto them was given power, as the scorpions of the earth have power.

Revelation 9:7-11 And the shapes of the locusts were like unto horses prepared unto battle; and on their heads were as it were crowns like gold, and their faces were as the faces of men. 8 And they had hair as the hair of women, and their teeth were as the teeth of lions. 9 And they had breastplates, as it were breastplates of iron; and the sound of their wings was as the sound of chariots of many horses running to battle. 10 And they had tails like unto scorpions, and there were stings in their tails: and their power was to hurt men five months. 11 And they had a king over them, which is the angel of the bottomless pit, whose name in the Hebrew tongue is Abaddon, but in the Greek tongue hath his name Apollyon.

Army #2 apparently from the pit also, released from an opening in the Euphrates River. There are 200,000,000 of these things. Something often overlooked, each creature holds a devil rider bringing their total number to 400,000,000. **Observe this army is led by four angels!** The devil horse-like creatures are composed of the following animals- horses, lions, serpents, and tails with heads. Their riders are not described, simply called *them that sat on them.* Again the Bible student should wonder how these creatures get into this condition.

Revelation 9:14-20 *Saying to the sixth angel which had the trumpet,* **Loose the four angels which are bound** *in the great river Euphrates.* **15** *And the four angels were loosed, which were prepared for an hour, and a day, and a month, and a year, for to slay the third part of men.* **16** *And the number of the army of the horsemen were two hundred thousand thousand: and I heard the number of them.* **17** *And thus I saw the horses in the vision,* **and them that sat on them***, having breastplates of fire, and of jacinth, and brimstone: and the heads of the horses were as the heads of lions; and out of their mouths issued fire and smoke and brimstone.* **18** *By these three was the third part of men killed, by the fire, and by the smoke, and by the brimstone, which issued out of their mouths.* **19** *For their power is in their mouth, and in their tails: for their tails were like unto serpents, and had heads, and with them they do hurt.* **20** *And the rest of the men which were not killed by these plagues yet repented not of the works of their hands, that they should not worship devils, and idols of gold, and silver, and brass, and stone, and of wood: which neither can see, nor hear, nor walk:*

Hypothesis

In the days of Noah, *Genesis 6*, angels biologically engineered the devil armies in *Revelation chapter 9*. Noah's Flood was a direct response to fallen angels altering biological DNA of men and animals to procreate new species. God imprisoned these genetic monstrosities under the earth where they have been reproducing ever since, and releases them during the Tribulation. The angels leading them are the same angels responsible for their existence. Peter and Jude refer to them as the angels that left their first estate and own habitation;

therefore, these exact angels fathered the giants. The significance of four angels discussed further in the chapter Identifying Angels.

Another primary correlation connects *Revelation 9 with Genesis 6.* While a variety of animals and insects combine to procreate these devils, one kind is missing. No marine life is represented. Read carefully *Genesis 6:7 and 7:21-23.*

God tells us specifically what types of life perished in the flood. All life on the face of the earth died. All creatures living on the dry land and breathed air died, an enormously important factor. It defines what did and did not survive the flood. God exempted marine life from judgment. Had the angels messed with the genome of aquatic life, the ark would have included an aquarium.

*Genesis 6:7 And the LORD said, I will destroy man whom I have created from **the face of the earth**; both man, and beast, and the creeping thing, and the fowls of the air; for it repenteth me that I have made them.*

*Genesis 7:21-23 And all flesh died that moved upon the earth, both of fowl, and of cattle, and of beast, and of every creeping thing that creepeth upon the earth, and every man: 22 **All in whose nostrils was the breath of life, of all that was in the dry land, died. 23** And every living substance was destroyed which was upon the face of the ground, both man, and cattle, and the creeping things, and the fowl of the heaven; and they were destroyed from the earth: and Noah only remained alive, and they that were with him in the ark.*

Giants Survive

§

ABOUT 1,000 YEARS AFTER NOAH's Flood during the days of Moses, giants appear again. The twelve spies sent into Canaan give testimony in *Numbers 13*.

Numbers 13:32-33 And they brought up an evil report of the land which they had searched unto the children of Israel, saying, The land, through which we have gone to search it, is a land that eateth up the inhabitants thereof; and all the people that we saw in it are men of a great stature. 33 And there we saw the giants, the sons of Anak, which come of the giants: and we were in our own sight as grasshoppers, and so we were in their sight.

IN THE DAYS OF NOAH, GOD SET FORTH SPECIFIC CRITERIA FOR JUDGMENT.

Genesis 7:22 All in whose nostrils was the breath of life, of all that was in the dry land, died.

All life on the face of the earth died. All creatures living on the dry land and breathed air died. *Genesis 7:22-* is very discriminating. Giants surviving the flood mean one of four things or a combination of these things:

1. Angels took women after the flood.
2. One of Noah's sons or their wives had genetic heredity to giants.
3. Giants can live underwater.
4. Giants capable of interplanetary mobility; they left earth and returned.
5. Giants survived under the earth.

Since God reacted so strongly to the sins precipitating the flood, I think it unlikely evil angels' married human women again so soon. Knowing God confined the other angels in hell, it would be rather stupid for an angel to take a wife. Therefore, it is my theory point #1 did not happen. However-based on *Genesis 6:4 and Matthew 24:37-39* everything happening in the days of Noah, *(all pre-flood activities)* happen again in the final generations before Jesus' return.

Point #2 also seems unlikely. As previously discussed, God segregated genetically pure and clean species on the ark. For God to preserve giants, or corrupt gene pools on the ark goes against the whole concept of ark preservation. Since God declares Noah *perfect in his generations*, corruption in his sons is not even possible; unless one includes Noah's wife's genetic heredity. Noah could be perfect, but his wife might not be. If one considers this idea, consider also the individual wives of Noah's three sons, Shem, Japheth, and Ham. The giant tribes appearing after the flood were genetically linked to Ham. The question for the Bible student- at what point did genetic tampering occur? Just because giants infiltrated Hamitic tribes, does not prove that Ham himself, or his wife carried the corrupt gene. 1000 years elapsed between Noah's flood and Joshua taking the land of Canaan. When angelic or giant corruption occurs is anyone's guess? If it happened generations after Noah's flood, then not all Ham's decedents need be affected. Alas, for me, *1 Timothy 1:4-* rapidly approaches. In conclusion, points 3,4, or 5 might explain giants surviving the flood.

Chapter Notes

1 Timothy 1:4 Neither give heed to fables and endless genealogies, which minister questions, rather than godly edifying which is in faith: so do.

Genesis 6:8-9 But Noah found grace in the eyes of the LORD. 9 These are the generations of Noah: Noah was a just man and perfect in his generations, and Noah walked with God.

*Genesis 6:4 There were giants in the earth in those days; **and also after that**, when the sons of God came in unto the daughters of men, and they bare children to them, the same became mighty men which were of old, men of renown.*

*Matthew 24:37-39 But **as the days of Noe were, so shall also the coming of the Son of man be.** 38 For as in the days that were before the flood they were eating and drinking, marrying and giving in marriage, until the day that Noe entered into the ark, **39** And knew not until the flood came, and took them all away; so shall also the coming of the Son of man be.*

*Ecclesiastes 1:9-10 The thing that hath been, it is that which shall be; and that which is done is that which shall be done: and there is no new thing under the sun. **10** Is there any thing whereof it may be said, See, this is new? it hath been already of old time, which was before us.*

Giant Culture

CAREFULLY READING *LEVITICUS CHAPTERS 18 and 20, and Numbers chapter 13*, reveal the giants' life style and culture in the land beyond Jordan. In these chapters, God gives numerous commands concerning behaviors he absolutely forbids. God's concluding statements on these laws provide the evidence for the way giants and the people lived. This knowledge also provides a righteous explanation as to why God ordered the annihilation of seven particular tribes. Without reproducing the entire chapters, a summary of giant behavior is given below:

GIANTS WERE:

- Cannibals
- Practiced human child sacrifice
- Worshipped Molech the fire god and idols
- Had sexual relations with animals
- Homosexuals
- Incestuous
- Adulterous

A SUMMARY:

Wicked angels, giants, and sinful people brought the whole human race and animal world to corruption in the days of Noah. Giants survived the flood (at least some of them) and continued their depraved lifestyles in the days of Moses. Indeed, the land of Canaan rivaled the days of Noah. God used the Jew, especially the army of Joshua to purge the land.

First generation giants were very important to Lucifer. Just think- an entirely new life form procreated by wicked angels, but still related to Adam. What a wondrous triumph for evil. Such creatures served Satan's ambitions in entirely new ways. Most likely Satan appointed himself step-father to the giants soon after God confined their angel daddies in Hell. Lucifer made sure they received a proper education in the powers of darkness. Satan used them to bring fallen mankind before his throne and serve and worship the creature rather than the creator.

With Noah's Flood came another victory for Satan, the destruction of billions of human beings. When the waters subsided, a new age began. Satan sought corruption of the new world through his own adopted ones, the giants. Infiltrating the descendants of Canaan, he reduced these peoples to a state rivaling Noah's generation. The land beyond the Jordan endured total defilement. But this time, God dealt with their abominations before they infected the whole world. Within time, giants realize the futility in continued war with God's people. Life on Earth is no longer tolerable for giants. So they hide, under the sea, or deep inside the earth, or on another planet.

CHAPTER NOTES

Leviticus 18:24-30 Defile not ye yourselves in any of these things: for in all these the nations are defiled which I cast out before you:

25 And the land is defiled: therefore I do visit the iniquity thereof upon it, and the land itself vomiteth out her inhabitants. 26 Ye shall therefore keep my statutes and my judgments, and shall not commit any of these abominations; neither any of your own nation, nor any stranger that sojourneth among you: 27 (For all these abominations have the men of the land done, which were before you, and the land is defiled;) 28 That the land spue not you out also, when ye defile it, as it spued out the nations that were before you. 29 For whosoever shall commit any of these abominations, even the souls that commit them shall be cut off from among their people. 30 Therefore shall ye keep mine ordinance, that ye commit not any one of these abominable customs, which were committed before you, and that ye defile not yourselves therein: I am the LORD your God.

Deuteronomy 9:1-5 Hear, O Israel: Thou art to pass over Jordan this day, to go in to possess nations greater and mightier than thyself, cities great and fenced up to heaven, 2 A people great and tall, the children of the Anakims, whom thou knowest, and of whom thou hast heard say, Who can stand before the children of Anak! 3 Understand therefore this day, that the LORD thy God is he which goeth over before thee; as a consuming fire he shall destroy them, and he shall bring them down before thy face: so shalt thou drive them out, and destroy them quickly, as the LORD hath said unto thee. 4 Speak not thou in thine heart, after that the LORD thy God hath cast them out from before thee, saying, For my righteousness the LORD hath brought me in to possess this land: but for the wickedness of these nations the LORD doth drive them out from before thee. 5 Not for thy righteousness, or for the uprightness of thine heart, dost thou go to possess their land: but for the wickedness of these nations the LORD thy God doth drive them out from before thee, and that he may perform the word which the LORD sware unto thy fathers, Abraham, Isaac, and Jacob.

Degeneration

§

IN THE DAYS OF NOAH, I suspect only a very few angels left their first estate and cohabitated with women; quite possibly four or five angels. And those being the same angels mentioned in *Revelation 9;* (discussed at length in the chapter Identifying Angels.) Angels procreated only the first generation giants; consequently, most the giants were fathered by the giants. Observing a degenerating process over the centuries supports this theory. The further away generations' get from the angels; giants get smaller and less intelligent.

OG AND GOLIATH

Compare Og, king of Bashan, over twelve feet tall- to Goliath who was only nine feet six inches tall. Goliath lived 450 years after Og. Og was slain around 1490 BC. Og's bed was nine cubits long and four cubits wide. (One cubit is 18 inches.) This translates into thirteen feet by six feet. A conservative estimate concludes Og's height over twelve feet tall. His weight would be harder to guess, perhaps 2,000 pounds or more? Scripture declares Og- the last of the giants. Since extraordinarily tall beings continued to exist, I conclude Og was a first generation giant; that is, a creature fathered directly by an angel.

King Og's kingdom consisted of more than sixty walled cities and many towns, well-built and well-defended. Such a kingdom reveals capable leadership with organized government.

Deuteronomy 3:11 For only Og king of Bashan remained of the remnant of giants; *behold, his bedstead was a bedstead of iron; is it not in Rabbath of the children of Ammon?* ***nine cubits was the length thereof, and four cubits the breadth of it,*** *after the cubit of a man.*

Deuteronomy 3:3-6 *So the LORD our God delivered into our hands Og also, the king of Bashan, and all his people: and we smote him until none was left to him remaining.* ***4*** *And we took all his cities at that time, there was not a city which we took not from them,* ***threescore cities, all the region of Argob, the kingdom of Og in Bashan. 5 All these cities were fenced with high walls, gates, and bars; beside unwalled towns a great many.*** ***6*** *And we utterly destroyed them, as we did unto Sihon king of Heshbon, utterly destroying the men, women, and children, of every city.*

GOLIATH

Approximately four hundred fifty years after Og, Goliath is on the scene *1st Samuel 17.* Considerably smaller than Og, Goliath measures six cubits and a span, or nine feet six inches. Not only is Goliath smaller than his ancestor, his intellectual abilities seem diminished. Raving against the Israeli army shows pride, but very little sense. Offering the servitude of the Philistines to hang in the balance over a battle between two men was stupid. Upon Goliath's death, pandemonium broke out within the ranks of the Philistines manifesting a lack of discipline and incompetent leadership. Goliath's abilities did not qualify him to run a kingdom. If he controlled anything (for he is called only a champion and not a king) it was a tribal army unit, and this he ruled by dominant physical strength.

As genetic nearness to the angels becomes more distant, giants become smaller and less intelligent. In fact, the Bible never even calls Goliath a giant-only people retelling the story do. Scripture declaring that only Og remained a remnant of the giants means Goliath cannot be a giant, in the technical/doctrinal sense. In other words, Goliath was not fathered directly by an angel; he was fathered by a giant.

1 Samuel 17:4 And there went out a champion out of the camp of the Philistines, named Goliath, of Gath, whose height was six cubits and a span.

1 Samuel 17:49-51 And David put his hand in his bag, and took thence a stone, and slang it, and smote the Philistine in his forehead, that the stone sunk into his forehead; and he fell upon his face to the earth. 50 So David prevailed over the Philistine with a sling and with a stone, and smote the Philistine, and slew him; but there was no sword in the hand of David. 51 Therefore David ran, and stood upon the Philistine, and took his sword, and drew it out of the sheath thereof, and slew him, and cut off his head therewith. And when the Philistines saw their champion was dead, they fled.

Deuteronomy 3:11 For only Og king of Bashan remained of the remnant of giants

GOLIATH FAMILY AND FRIENDS
Considering *2nd Samuel 21:16-22 and 1st Chronicles 20:4-8.*

Carefully considering these texts begs the question, is the giant in Gath and Goliath the Gittite the same person? If he is than Goliath fathered his four sons through his own mother, thus he would be their father and brother. And considering the sexual permissiveness and debased religious doctrines of Molech, this is a possibility. On the other hand, the giant in Gath could be the father of Goliath and his four brothers. Verse twenty-two does not declare the giant had only four sons; he could have had more. Does 21:16 positively identify the giant in Gath as Goliath? We were never told Goliath's spear weighed three hundred shekels of brass. Scripture informs his spear head weighed three hundred shekels of iron *1st Samuel 17:7.* Therefore the giant in Gath could still be alive after David and his mighty men took care of his five boys.

Is Ishibibenob the son of Goliath as verse sixteen and twenty-two implies? The staff being like a weavers beam directly correlates to *1st Samuel 17:7.* A Gittite is an inhabitant of Gath, here is the man whom David slew with a stone and a sword. And the same is a brother to the four sons of the giant in Gath.

Most importantly, *2nd Samuel 21:20-* shows giants degenerating. Six fingers, six toes signal a genetic problem. Perhaps the Lord is assuring giants stop mingling their seed with the daughters of men. Either way, giants have their problems. God commissions the Jews as his official giant killers and is ensuring the Hebrews win every battle.

*2 Samuel 21:16-22 And **Ishbibenob, which was of the sons of the giant,** the weight of whose spear **weighed three hundred shekels of brass in weight,** he being girded with a new sword, thought to have slain David. **17** But Abishai the son of Zeruiah succoured him, and smote the Philistine, and killed him. Then the men of David sware unto him, saying, Thou shalt go no more out with us to battle, that thou quench not the light of Israel. **18** And it came to pass after this, that there was again a battle with the Philistines at Gob: then Sibbechai the Hushathite slew Saph, which was of the sons of the giant. **19** And there was again a battle in Gob with the Philistines, where Elhanan the son of Jaareoregim, a Bethlehemite, **slew the brother of Goliath the Gittite, the staff of whose spear was like a weaver's beam. 20** And there was yet a battle in Gath, where was a man of great stature, that had on every hand six fingers, and on every foot six toes, four and twenty in number; and he also was born to the giant.*

21 And when he defied Israel, Jonathan the son of Shimea the brother of David slew him. **22 These four were born to the giant in Gath,** *and fell by the hand of David, and by the hand of his servants.*

   1 Chronicles 20:4-8 *And it came to pass after this, that there arose war at Gezer with the Philistines; at which time Sibbechai the Hushathite slew Sippai, that was of the children of the giant: and they were subdued. 5 And there was war again with the Philistines; and Elhanan the son of Jair slew Lahmi the brother of Goliath the Gittite, whose spear staff was like a weaver's beam. 6 And yet again there was war at Gath,* **where was a man of great stature, whose fingers and toes were four and twenty, six on each hand, and six on each foot: and he also was the son of the giant.** *7 But when he defied Israel, Jonathan the son of Shimea David's brother slew him.* **8 These were born unto the giant in Gath;** *and they fell by the hand of David, and by the hand of his servants.*

Naming Angels

§

ANAK AND ARBA

DOES THE BIBLE GIVE US the names of the fallen angels who precipitated the flood? Nearly a thousand years after *Genesis 6*, giants show up again. Consider Anak the giant. When Moses sent twelve men to spy out the Promised Land, ten of them returned very concerned about the sons of Anak *Numbers 13:17-33*.

*Numbers 13:31-33 But the men that went up with him said, We be not able to go up against the people; for they are stronger than we. 32 And they brought up an evil report of the land which they had searched unto the children of Israel, saying, The land, through which we have gone to search it, is a land that eateth up the inhabitants thereof; and all the people that we saw in it are men of a great stature. 33 And there **we saw the giants, the sons of Anak, which come of the giants:** and we were in our own sight as grasshoppers, and so we were in their sight.*

Anak was a patriarch, his people, the Anakims, the most prevalent giant tribe in scripture. Although no records show Anak alive in the days of Noah or the days of Moses, there is no record of his death either

Among the ten giants the Bible recognizes by name (including Goliath) are Anak's three sons- Sheshai, Talmai, and Ahiman. These three were probably leaders in the land of Canaan. The city of Arba, also called Kirjatharba and Hebron, served as the capital of the giant world until Caleb drove them out scattering a remnant to the cities of Gath, Gaza, and Ashod. **Interestingly Anak's father, Arba, is never identified as a giant, rather, he is only called a man.** This merits a careful investigation. It is very puzzling the Jews identified giants with Anak, but not with Anak's father, Arba.

*Joshua 15:13-14 And unto Caleb the son of Jephunneh he gave a part among the children of Judah, according to the commandment of the LORD to Joshua, even the **city of Arba the father of Anak**, which city is Hebron. 14 And Caleb drove thence the three sons of Anak, Sheshai, and Ahiman, and Talmai, **the children of Anak.***

*Joshua 14:15 And the name of Hebron before was Kirjatharba; **which Arba was a great man among the Anakims**. And the land had rest from war.*

The Bible identifies Arba as Anak's father. He is also called a great man. The city of Arba is capital of the giant world. All of this is more than curious: Why didn't the twelve spies report they had seen the sons of Arba- rather than the sons of Anak? Shouldn't a man important enough to name a capital city after, and a man declared *great* be identified as the father of the tribe?

Not if Arba is an angel! And Anak was a first generation giant. Logically, Anak identifies as the patriarch, because he would be the first giant. His father, Arba, the angel is a regular sized man. I believe this to be exactly the case. Remember four angels lead the devil army in *Revelation 9.* The name **Arba interpreted means *one of four.*** All this corroborative evidence seems conclusive, Arba is an angel; he is one of the four angels leading a devil army in the Tribulation.

*Revelation 9:13-16 And the sixth angel sounded, and I heard a voice from the four horns of the golden altar which is before God, 14 Saying to the sixth angel which had the trumpet, **Loose the four angels which are***

bound in the great river Euphrates. 15 And the four angels were loosed, *which were prepared for an hour, and a day, and a month, and a year, for to slay the third part of men.* **16** *And the number of the army of the horsemen were two hundred thousand thousand: and I heard the number of them.*

These four angels, clearly evil, because they are bound and imprisoned. These same four angels lead the devil army of 400,000,000, the army made up of genetically confused creatures. What a fitting command if these same angels (sons of God) engineered their confusion.

The Other Three Angels

Do we know the names of the other three angels released from the Euphrates? The king of the bottomless pit is an angel named Apollyon. **Apollyon** is already out of the pit and controlling the first devil army when God releases the additional four angels. *Revelation 9:15* which means the four angels control the second devil army released in Revelation chapter 9.

Revelation 9:10-11 *And they had tails like unto scorpions, and there were stings in their tails: and their power was to hurt men five months.* **11** *And they had a king over them, which is the angel of the bottomless pit, whose name in the Hebrew tongue is* **Abaddon, but in the Greek tongue hath his name Apollyon.**

Naming the other angels is admittedly speculative. **Consider Hinnom.** A character never personally described, but mentioned as the father of a person named for the valley of the giants. Much like Arba, the emphasis is on his son. The valley is a focal point for the horrible giant rituals of child sacrifice. **The clue, here, is the valley is not called after Hinnom, but after his giant son.** The name Hinnom is in the Bible 13 times. Hinnom interpreted means *"to make self-drowsy: behold them"*.

Joshua 18:16 *And the border came down to the end of the mountain that lieth before the valley of the* **son of Hinnom, and which is in the valley of the giants** *on the north, and descended to the valley of Hinnom, to the side of Jebusi on the south, and descended to Enrogel,*

2 Chronicles 33:6 *And he caused his children to pass through the fire in the valley* **of the son of Hinnom:** *also he observed times, and used enchantments, and used witchcraft, and dealt with a familiar spirit, and with wizards: he wrought much evil in the sight of the LORD, to provoke him to anger.*

Another name associated with Hinnom is **Tophet**. Indeed, Tophet is the high place or worship center inside the valley of the son of Hinnom. Tophet was the actual place where they slaughtered children. From *Isaiah 30:33*, we learn Tophet is an ancient king whom God meets in judgment. Tophet interpreted means *"spititng: object of contempt"*.

Jeremiah 7:31-33 *And they have built the* **high places of Tophet, which is in the valley of the son of Hinnom,** *to burn their sons and their daughters in the fire; which I commanded them not, neither came it into my heart.* **32** *Therefore, behold, the days come, saith the LORD, that it shall no more be called Tophet, nor the valley of the son of Hinnom, but the valley of slaughter: for they shall bury in Tophet, till there be no place.* **33** *And the carcases of this people shall be meat for the fowls of the heaven, and for the beasts of the earth; and none shall fray them away.*

Isaiah 30:33 **For Tophet is ordained of old; yea, for the king it** *is prepared; he hath made it deep and large: the pile thereof is fire and much wood; the breath of the LORD, like a stream of brimstone, doth kindle it.*

Still another is Molech *the king, shame or shameful king.* Molech is a false God worshipped by giants and peoples influenced by giants. Molech demanded child sacrifice. When God speaks about Molech, he seems to be speaking about an actual person as opposed to just an idol.

Leviticus 20:2-3 *Again, thou shalt say to the children of Israel, Whosoever he be of the children of Israel, or of the strangers that sojourn in*

*Israel, **that giveth any of his seed unto Molech;** he shall surely be put to death: the people of the land shall stone him with stones. **3** And I will set my face against that man, and will cut him off from among his people; because **he hath given of his seed unto Molech,** to defile my sanctuary, and to profane my holy name.*

*Jeremiah 32:35 And they built the high places of Baal, **which are in the valley of the son of Hinnom, to cause their sons and their daughters to pass through the fire unto Molech;** which I commanded them not, neither came it into my mind, that they should do this abomination, to cause Judah to sin.*

Revelation 9:14 Saying to the sixth angel which had the trumpet, Loose the four angels which are bound in the great river Euphrates.

Revelation 9:11 And they had a king over them, which is the angel of the bottomless pit, whose name in the Hebrew tongue is Abaddon, but in the Greek tongue hath his name Apollyon.

CHAPTER NOTES

Ten giants mentioned by name:

1.Og	2.Anak	3.Sheshai	4.Talmai
5.Ahiman	6.Goliath	7.*Ishbibenob*	
8.*Saph*	9.*Sippai,*	10.*Lahmi*	

Giant Tribes: Anakims, Zamzummims, Emims, Horims, Avimims
Main Giant texts: *Deuteronomy 2, Joshua 14,15; 2 Samuel 21, 1 Chronicles 20*

Fallen Angels: Apollyon, Arba, Hinnom, Tophet, Molech

One World Government

§

AN OFTEN OVERLOOKED FACT IS Noah lived 350 years after the flood; therefore, the days of Noah include 350 years this side of the flood. Clearly likening the last days' to Noah's generation places emphasis on Genesis 6's societal conditions, fallen angels, giants, and moral depravity; however this final era of Noah's life should not be ignored. The most significant event of Noah's last 350 years was the political, attempt to establish a one world government. Nimrod orchestrated building Babel. Noah was a citizen of Babel.

Genesis 9:28-29 And Noah lived after the flood three hundred and fifty years. 29 And all the days of Noah were nine hundred and fifty years: and he died.

One hundred years after Noah's Flood a charismatic leader, Nimrod, attempted to establish a one world government. Nimrod organized the entire existing human race to build a city, Babel. He also organized a building project of a tower intended to reach heaven. The one world government is not the primary focus of this study, but it is a condition of the days of Noah. The political consequences of last day prophecies and a careful consideration of Babylon, see chapter *Daniel's fourth kingdom*.

Genesis 10:8-10 And Cush begat Nimrod: he began to be a mighty one in the earth. 9 He was a mighty hunter before the LORD: wherefore it is said, *Even as Nimrod the mighty hunter before the LORD.* **10** *And the beginning of his kingdom was Babel, and Erech, and Accad, and Calneh, in the land of Shinar.*

Genesis 11:1-6 ***And the whole earth was of one language, and of one speech. 2 And it came to pass, as they journeyed from the east, that they found a plain in the land of Shinar; and they dwelt there.*** *3 And they said one to another, Go to, let us make brick, and burn them throughly. And they had brick for stone, and slime had they for morter.* **4** *And they said, Go to, let us build us a city and a tower, whose top may reach unto heaven; and let us make us a name, lest we be scattered abroad upon the face of the whole earth.* **5** *And the LORD came down to see the city and the tower, which the children of men builded.* **6** *And the LORD said, Behold, the people is one, and they have all one language; and this they begin to do: and now nothing will be restrained from them, which they have imagined to do.*

HISTORICAL ANALYSIS

NEW TESTAMENT WARNING

The first chapter in Romans provides historical commentary on the days of Noah. Apostle Paul discusses hard truth and consequences for sin. But his comments also depict a society in the past, a society God *gave up*. Presently, 2002, we live in the Church Age, God has not given this world up- All persons living in this dispensation can be saved by putting their faith in Jesus Christ. Notice the people, given up, absolutely know the truth. These people are not ignorant to God's grace; they rejected the Lord; there were no unreached people in the antediluvian world.

Romans 1:18-32 *For the wrath of God is revealed from heaven against all ungodliness and unrighteousness of men,* ***who hold the truth***

*in unrighteousness; 19 Because that which may be known of God is manifest in them; **for God hath shewed it unto them.** 20 For the invisible things of him from the creation of the world are clearly seen, being understood by the things that are made, even his eternal power and Godhead; so that they are without excuse:*

Notice in verse 21, the narrative becomes very discriminating; God discusses a particular group of people who lived in the past. Certainly spiritual applications to modern times, but doctrinally these are the days of Noah. The people God gave up were much more than homosexuals. These people willingly made an image of the creature to worship. Consciously and with freewill, they replaced the true God for an image and worshipped Satan. Although this sounds like what happens in the Tribulation, it also happened in the days of Noah.

ANTEDILUVIANS' LIFESTYLE MANIFEST

*Romans 21 Because that, **when they knew God,** they glorified him not as God, neither were thankful; but became vain in their imaginations, and their foolish heart was darkened. 22 Professing themselves to be wise, they became fools, 23 And changed the glory of the uncorruptible God into an image made like to corruptible man, and to birds, and fourfooted beasts, and creeping things. 24 **Wherefore God also gave them up** to uncleanness through the lusts of their own hearts, to dishonour their own bodies between themselves: 25 Who changed the truth of God into a lie, and worshipped and served the creature more than the Creator, who is blessed for ever. Amen. 26 **For this cause God gave them up unto vile affections:** for even their women did change the natural use into that which is against nature: 27 And likewise also the men, leaving the natural use of the woman, burned in their lust one toward another; men with men working that which is unseemly, and receiving in themselves that recompence of* *their error which was meet.* **28** *And even as they did not like to retain God in their knowledge, God gave them over to a reprobate mind, to do those things which are not convenient;* **29-Being filled with all unrighteousness, fornication, wickedness, covetousness, maliciousness; full of envy, murder, debate, deceit, malignity; whisperers, 30 Backbiters, haters of God, despiteful, proud, boasters, inventors of evil things, disobedient to parents, 31 Without understanding, covenantbreakers, without natural affection, implacable, unmerciful: 32 Who knowing the judgment of God, that they which commit such things are worthy of death, not only do the same, but have pleasure in them that do them.**

Ecclesiastes 3:15 *That which hath been is now; and that which is to be hath already been; and God requireth that which is past.*

Things under Earth

§

THINGS LIVING UNDER THE EARTH may seem more like science fiction than a topic for Bible study, but God tells us plainly life exists inside the earth. Certainly hell's occupants are under the earth. Revelation 9 documents two massive subterranean devil armies which emerge out of the earth during the Tribulation. Just think over 400,000,000 inhuman things under the earth- just waiting to come up. And the evil angels from Genesis 6, God confined them under the earth. Quite honestly, more goes on underground than most people care to know; however not all things under the earth are evil.

WHAT HAPPENED TO THE GARDEN OF EDEN?

With only casual investigation, the Garden of Eden disappears into obscurity. One could presume God's curse on the earth simply ravished the garden of God into regular terrain. But several scriptures indicate God preserved the Garden of Eden deep inside the earth.

The Garden of Eden, Paradise, and Abraham's bosom are synonymous; in other words they are all the same place. This assertion, of course, needs to be proved with scripture.

Before Jesus' resurrection, the souls of saved people went to a literal place called Abraham's bosom, a place so wonderful God also

called it paradise. Jesus taught that hell and paradise are geographically located side by side. The familiar passage concerning Lazarus
and the rich man provides evidence. *Luke 16* gives a visual percep-
tion of the inner earth's geography.

*Luke 16:20-26 And there was a certain beggar named Lazarus,
which was laid at his gate, full of sores, 21 And desiring to be fed with
the crumbs which fell from the rich man's table: moreover the dogs came
and licked his sores. 22 And it came to pass, that the beggar died, and was
carried by the angels into Abraham's bosom: the rich man also died,
and was buried; 23 **And in hell he lift up his eyes, being in torments,
and seeth Abraham afar off, and Lazarus in his bosom.** 24 And he
cried and said, Father Abraham, have mercy on me, and send Lazarus,
that he may dip the tip of his finger in water, and cool my tongue; for I am
tormented in this flame. 25 But Abraham said, Son, remember that thou
in thy lifetime receivedst thy good things, and likewise Lazarus evil things:
but now he is comforted, and thou art tormented. 26 And beside all this,
**between us and you there is a great gulf fixed: so that they which
would pass from hence to you cannot;** neither can they pass to us, that
would come from thence.*

For illustration; think of the earth as a house, and the ground
you're standing on as the roof. Remove the roof and several rooms
appear. The most beautiful room would be Abraham's bosom. As
Jesus hung on the cross dying for our sins, one of the men crucified
with him repented and believed in Christ. Jesus promised they would
be together in paradise that very same day. Jesus calling the place par-
adise- proves paradise is synonymous with Abraham's bosom.

*Luke 23:42-43 And he said unto Jesus, Lord, remember me when
thou comest into thy kingdom. 43 And Jesus said unto him, Verily I say
unto thee, **To day shalt thou be with me in paradise.***

Jesus was dead 3 days. Jesus spent those 3 days inside the earth.
If the repentant sinner on the cross was with Jesus the same day he

died, then they were somewhere inside the earth. Jesus did not ascend into heaven until after 3 days.

Matthew 12:40 *For as Jonas was three days and three nights in the whale's belly; so shall the Son of man be three days and three nights in the heart of the earth.*

God created the Garden of Eden in a great, beautiful valley. After the fall, God sealed the valley over with land. This means Eden is still where it always was - but now we can't see it because it's buried inside the earth. Consider Ezekiel chapter 31. The passage is loaded, but for the purpose of this study, focus only on geography. The Garden of God is now in the nether parts of the earth. The Garden of Eden and Paradise, and Abraham's bosom are the same place.

Ezekiel 31:8-18 *The cedars **in the garden of God** could not hide him: the fir trees were not like his boughs, and the chesnut trees were not like his branches; nor **any tree in the garden of God** was like unto him in his beauty. **9** I have made him fair by the multitude of his branches: so that all the trees of Eden, that were in the garden of God, envied him. **10** Therefore thus saith the Lord GOD; Because thou hast lifted up thyself in height, and he hath shot up his top among the thick boughs, and his heart is lifted up in his height; **11** I have therefore delivered him into the hand of the mighty one of the heathen; he shall surely deal with him: I have driven him out for his wickedness. **12** And strangers, the terrible of the nations, have cut him off, and have left him: upon the mountains and in all the valleys his branches are fallen, and his boughs are broken by all the rivers of the land; and all the people of the earth are gone down from his shadow, and have left him. **13** Upon his ruin shall all the fowls of the heaven remain, and all the beasts of the field shall be upon his branches: **14 To the end that none of all the trees by the waters exalt themselves for their height, neither shoot up their top among the thick boughs, neither their trees stand up in their height, all that drink water: for they are all delivered unto death, to the nether parts of the earth, in the***

midst of the children of men, with them that go down to the pit. 15 Thus saith the Lord GOD; In the day when he went down to the grave I caused a mourning: I covered the deep for him, and I restrained the floods thereof, and the great waters were stayed: and I caused Lebanon to mourn for him, and all the trees of the field fainted for him. 16 I made the nations to shake at the sound of his fall, when I cast him down to hell with them that descend into the pit: and all the trees of Eden, the choice and best of Lebanon, all that drink water, shall be comforted in the nether parts of the earth. 17 They also went down into hell with him unto them that be slain with the sword; and they that were his arm, that dwelt under his shadow in the midst of the heathen. 18 To whom art thou thus like in glory and in greatness among the trees of Eden? yet shalt thou be brought down with the trees of Eden unto the nether parts of the earth: thou shalt lie in the midst of the uncircumcised with them that be slain by the sword. This is Pharaoh and all his multitude, saith the Lord GOD.

Notice in verse *31:16-* this inner earth cavity contains a sanctuary of comfort. And *comfort* is not a word associated with torments of hell. In fact, the same word is used in *Luke 16:25* -for Lazarus in paradise. The saved souls go down into the earth to be comforted, and the lost souls go down into the earth to hell. Both regions exist in the nether parts of the earth. Paradise is geographically located next to hell, just as Jesus taught in the story of Lazarus and the rich man, Luke 16.

PARADISE

The word paradise is in the Bible three times. The first time paradise is mentioned Jesus speaks to the malefactor on the cross, "to day thou shalt be with me in paradise." As previously mentioned Jesus called Abraham's bosom, paradise.

Luke 23:43 And Jesus said unto him, Verily I say unto thee, **To day shalt thou be with me in paradise.**

The second mention of paradise is in 2 Corinthians. Apostle Paul is caught up to a paradise located in the third heaven.

2 Corinthians 12:4 How that **he was caught up into paradise,** *and heard unspeakable words, which it is not lawful for a man to utter.*

Jesus led captivity captive out of paradise, the captive believers temporarily housed in the nether earth paradise until Jesus paid for their sins on the cross. This all coincides perfectly with the doctrine of Abraham's bosom and the repentant malefactor who died with Jesus.

Ephesians 4:8-10 Wherefore he saith, When he ascended up on high, he led captivity captive, and gave gifts unto men. 9 (Now that he ascended, what is it but that he also descended first into the lower parts of the earth? 10 He that descended is the same also that ascended up far above all heavens, that he might fill all things.)

Because of that wondrous exodus, many Bible students presume paradise is now empty, and/or paradise itself was taken to the third heaven. But a paradise in heaven is no reason to conclude the paradise inside the earth is gone. Several earthly locations have a heavenly parallel.

1. There is a Jerusalem on earth and a Jerusalem in heaven.
2. There was a temple on earth and a temple in heaven.
3. There is a Mt. Zion on earth and a Mt. Zion in heaven.
4. There is also a paradise in earth and paradise in heaven.

The third and final mention of paradise is in Revelation. *Revelation 2:7* provides definitive text. The tree of life is in the Garden of Eden; thus Eden is paradise.

Revelation 2:7 He that hath an ear, let him hear what the Spirit saith unto the churches; **To him that overcometh will I give to eat of the tree of life, which is in the midst of the paradise of God.**

The tree of life shows up again in the Millennium and then again in eternity. *Revelation 22:2.* The tree of life is always on earth. God intended the tree of life for Adam and Eve and their children to get everlasting physical life- Not for the Bride of Jesus Christ (Christians) who receive eternal life at salvation- and everlasting physical life at the rapture. God had a reason for making the tree of life, and he had a reason for putting it in the Garden of Eden. God has not changed his mind.

Genesis 2:8-9 And the LORD God planted a garden eastward in Eden; and there he put the man whom he had formed. 9 And out of the ground made the LORD God to grow every tree that is pleasant to the sight, and good for food; ***the tree of life also in the midst of the garden,*** *and the tree of knowledge of good and evil.*

THE REAPPEARANCE OF EDEN

When Jesus Christ returns at the end of the Tribulation, he touches down on the Mount of Olives. The earth opens revealing a very great valley, exposing the nether earth and the Garden of Eden.

Zechariah 14:4 And his feet shall stand in that day upon the mount of Olives, which is before Jerusalem on the east, ***and the mount of Olives shall cleave in the midst thereof toward the east and toward the west, and there shall be a very great valley; and half of the mountain shall remove toward the north, and half of it toward the south.***

In the Millennium, the earth opens and the glorious treasures buried inside become visible. This wondrous reappearing of an inner earth is prophesied by Isaiah. The Garden of Eden was originally in a valley, and then God covered the valley with land. The tree of life is still there awaiting its original intention. The tree of life provides eternal life to an endless dispensation of God's people yet to be born. The earth opening reveals paradise lost.

Isaiah 45:8 Drop down, ye heavens, from above, and let the skies pour down righteousness: **let the earth open,** and let them bring forth salvation, and let righteousness spring up together; I the LORD have created it.

The scene is beautiful. Jesus returns with his saints from the 3rd heaven, and the earth opens and righteousness comes from below. Ponder the statement, *"and let them bring forth salvation"* Who is them? What is this salvation and righteousness that *spring up?* As the geographical regeneration continues; the changes are staggering. See also *Ezekiel 47.*

Isaiah 44:23 Sing, O ye heavens; for the LORD hath done it: shout, **ye lower parts of the earth:** break forth into singing, ye mountains, O forest, and every tree therein: for the LORD hath redeemed Jacob, and glorified himself in Israel.

Philippians 2:10 That at the name of Jesus every knee should bow, of things in heaven, and things in earth, **and things under the earth;**

Revelation 5:13 And every creature which is in heaven, and on the earth, **and under the earth,** and such as are in the sea, and all that are in them, heard I saying, Blessing, and honour, and glory, and power, be unto him that sitteth upon the throne, and unto the Lamb for ever and ever.

Zechariah 14:9-10 And the LORD shall be king over all the earth: in that day shall there be one LORD, and his name one. **10** All the land shall be turned as a plain from Geba to Rimmon south of Jerusalem: **and it shall be lifted up, and inhabited in her place,** from Benjamin's gate unto the place of the first gate, unto the corner gate, and from the tower of Hananeel unto the king's winepresses.

REGENERATION, REST, REFRESHING

The period Christians call the Millennium is biblically referred to as the **Regeneration, Times of Refreshing, the Kingdom Age, and the Rest.** After what the earth endured in Tribulation, these words perfectly describe what's happening to the planet. When Jesus touches down on the Mount of Olives, the earth's regeneration begins (Mt. 19:28) the times of refreshing arrive (Acts 3:19), and believers and the earth enjoy a 1000 year dispensation of rest (Hebrews 4:9). Indeed this old earth, ravished by abuse, pollution, tribulation, constant war, etc. is in great need of some "R&R" And God begins a process of restoration during the Millennium, this old earth starts to heal.

Matthew 19:28 *And Jesus said unto them, Verily I say unto you, That ye which have followed me,* **in the regeneration when the Son of man shall sit in the throne of his glory,** *ye also shall sit upon twelve thrones, judging the twelve tribes of Israel.*

Acts 3:19-21 *Repent ye therefore, and be converted, that your sins may be blotted out,* **when the times of refreshing shall come from the presence of the Lord; 20** *And he shall send Jesus Christ, which before was preached unto you:* **21** *Whom the heaven must receive until the times of restitution of all things, which God hath spoken by the mouth of all his holy prophets since the world began.*

Hebrews 4:9 *There remaineth therefore* **a rest to** *the people of God.*

In the future, Jerusalem is the capital of the earth; also the capital of the universe, the exact place where God puts His Temple and His throne. Jesus Christ rules the entire universe from Jerusalem. Remember, *Isaiah 9:7* declares the Lord's government increases in size forever. Earth, then, is only the beginning.

Presently the city of Zion (heaven's Jerusalem) and God's Temple, and his throne exist in the 3rd Heaven, a cosmographical location called the sides of the north. As the Millennium continues, the earth's geographical regeneration is staggering. At this time, heaven's Zion and God's Temple set down in Israel. Observe God actually transplants geography and architecture from the 3rd heaven and places them in Israel.

Ezekiel 37:26-27 *Moreover I will make a covenant of peace with them; it shall be an everlasting covenant with them: and I will place them, and multiply them, and will set my sanctuary in the midst of them for evermore. 27 My tabernacle also shall be with them: yea, I will be their God, and they shall be my people.*

Hebrews 13:14 *For here have we no continuing city, but we seek one to come.*

Galatians 4:26 *But Jerusalem which is above is free, which is the mother of us all.*

Ezekiel 43:7 *And he said unto me, Son of man, the place of my throne, and the place of the soles of my feet, where I will dwell in the midst of the children of Israel for ever, and my holy name, shall the house of Israel no more defile, neither they, nor their kings, by their whoredom, nor by the carcases of their kings in their high places.*

Isaiah 2:1-5 *The word that Isaiah the son of Amoz saw concerning Judah and Jerusalem.* **2 And it shall come to pass in the last days, that the mountain of the LORD'S house shall be established in the top of the mountains, and shall be exalted above the hills; and all nations shall flow unto it.** *3 And many people shall go and say, Come ye, and let us go up to the mountain of the LORD, to the house of the God of Jacob; and he will teach us of his ways, and we will walk in his paths: for out of Zion shall go forth the law, and the word of the LORD from Jerusalem. 4 And he shall judge among the nations, and shall rebuke many people: and they shall beat their swords into plowshares, and their spears into pruninghooks: nation shall not lift up sword against nation, neither shall they learn war any more. 5 O house of Jacob, come ye, and let us walk in the light of the LORD.*

Psalm 48:1-2 *A Song and Psalm for the sons of Korah. Great is the LORD, and greatly to be praised in the city of our God, in the mountain of his holiness. 2 Beautiful for situation, the joy of the whole earth, is mount Zion, on the sides of the north, the city of the great King.*

Grapes and Blood

§

THROUGHOUT THE BIBLE, GOD MAKES some very interesting and sometimes peculiar statements about grapes. Most importantly, grapes associate with blood. The foundation for grapes being a type or symbol of blood is established in the Old Testament.

*Genesis 49:11 Binding his foal unto the vine, and his ass's colt unto the choice vine; he washed his garments in wine, and his **clothes in the blood of grapes:***

*Deuteronomy 32:14 Butter of kine, and milk of sheep, with fat of lambs, and rams of the breed of Bashan, and goats, with the fat of kidneys of wheat; and thou didst drink **the pure blood of the grape.***

Pure grape juice (being a type of blood) is consistent with New Testament typology, especially as it applies to the Lord's Supper, also referred to as Communion in some churches. Jesus identified grape juice as a symbol of his blood for the Lord's Supper.

*Matthew 26:27-29 And he took **the cup,** and gave thanks, and gave it to them, saying, Drink ye all of it; 28 **For this is my blood of the new testament,** which is shed for many for the remission of sins. 29 But I say unto you, I will not drink henceforth of this fruit of the vine, until that day when I drink it new with you in my Father's kingdom.*

MANY CHURCHES USE WINE INSTEAD OF PURE GRAPE JUICE FOR COMMUNION. DOES IT MATTER?

Examining the passages concerning the Lord's Supper, we learn God never uses the word *wine*. Every time the Bible address the drink used in Communion, the terminology is *the cup- or the fruit of the vine.*

Once grape juice ferments, it is no longer pure. The fermentation process destroys the purity, thus wine cannot be a type of Jesus' blood. Just as leavened bread is inappropriate for Communion bread, fermented grape juice or wine is inappropriate to symbolize Jesus' blood. Interestingly, one could make the case alcoholic wine is a type of man's corrupted blood; therefore, using wine for Communion is a mistake.

DON'T COMPLICATE THE ISSUE

Some Christians, who correctly oppose using wine for the Lord's Supper, try and strengthen their position by adding an additional argument that new wine does not have any alcohol content. Their argument is founded in *Isaiah 65:8-* where the verse declares new wine is found in the cluster. Their logic being- if new wine is literally in grapes growing on the vine, then it can't have alcohol in it. But the argument is unnecessary and a distraction. It puts the emphasis on a debate over when is juice wine. Why debate the definition of a word God isn't even using? Wine is not the pure blood of the grape- the pure blood of the grape is juice.

Throughout the Bible, God uses the word *wine* -212 times. But God- never uses the word wine in regards to the Lord's Supper. Neither new wine nor old wine is mentioned; the terms used are cup or fruit of the vine.

Luke 22:17-20 *And he took the cup, and gave thanks, and said, Take this, and divide it among yourselves:* **18** *For I say unto you, I will not drink of the fruit of the vine, until the kingdom of God shall come.* **19** *And he took bread, and gave thanks, and brake it, and gave unto them, saying, This is my body which is given for you: this do in remembrance of me.* **20** *Likewise also the cup after supper, saying, This cup is the new testament in my blood, which is shed for you.*

Mark 14:23-25 *And he took the cup, and when he had given thanks, he gave it to them: and they all drank of it.* **24** *And he said unto them, This is my blood of the new testament, which is shed for many.* **25** *Verily I say unto you, I will drink no more of the fruit of the vine, until that day that I drink it new in the kingdom of God.*

1 Corinthians 11:25-26 *After the same manner also he took the cup, when he had supped, saying, This cup is the new testament in my blood: this do ye, as oft as ye drink it, in remembrance of me.* **26** *For as often as ye eat this bread, and drink this cup, ye do shew the Lord's death till he come.*

UNLEAVENED BREAD

The same logic of using uncorrupted juice applies to the bread. Jesus instructed his disciples to use bread to symbolically represent his body. But not just any bread. Bread made with leaven (yeast) is not used because leaven represents sin. Jesus' body was not corrupted or sinful. By the way, leaven is usually used in making wine.

John 6:47-48 *Verily, verily, I say unto you, He that believeth on me hath everlasting life.* **48** *I am that bread of life.*

1 Corinthians 5:6-8 *Your glorying is not good. Know ye not that a little leaven leaveneth the whole lump?* **7** *Purge out therefore the old leaven, that ye may be a new lump, as ye are unleavened. For even Christ our passover is sacrificed for us:* **8** *Therefore let us keep the feast, not with* *old leaven, neither with the leaven of malice and wickedness; but with the unleavened bread of sincerity and truth.*

Exodus 34:25 Thou shalt not offer the blood of my sacrifice with leaven; neither shall the sacrifice of the feast of the passover be left unto the morning.

THE NAZARITE VOW

No information about grapes is more fascinating or mysterious than the vow of the Nazarite. The doctrinal criterion for the Nazarite's vow is found in *Numbers 6*. God absolutely forbids grapes to the Nazarite. During the Nazarite's time of separation, grapes, in all forms are off limits.

*Numbers 6:1-6 And the LORD spake unto Moses, saying, 2 Speak unto the children of Israel, and say unto them, When either man or woman shall separate themselves to vow a vow of a Nazarite, to separate themselves unto the LORD: 3 He shall **separate himself from wine and strong drink, and shall drink no vinegar of wine, or vinegar of strong drink, neither shall he drink any liquor of grapes, nor eat moist grapes, or dried.** 4 All the days of his separation shall he eat nothing that is made of the vine tree, from the kernels even to the husk. 5 All the days of the vow of his separation there shall **no rasor come upon his head:** until the days be fulfilled, in the which he separateth himself unto the LORD, he shall be holy, and shall let the locks of the hair of his head grow. 6 All the days that he separateth himself unto the LORD **he shall come at no dead body.***

Observe Nazarites, not only forbidden grapes and wine, they couldn't even eat raisins! Also, they were not allowed to cut their hair, nor were they allowed to go near any dead body. No doubt, it is the Nazarite's vow which forms the basis for the theory Jesus had long hair. But once again, a careful reading should clear up any private interpretations. Jesus is a Nazarene not a Nazarite. A Nazarene was a person whose residence was from the town of Nazareth. A

Nazarite was someone who had taken a vow pledging specific dietary observances, as well as other behaviors.

JESUS IS A NAZARENE NOT A NAZARITE.

Matthew 2:23 And he came and dwelt in a city called Nazareth: that it might be fulfilled which was spoken by the prophets, He shall be called a Nazarene.

Jesus' actions while on earth conflict with the Nazarite's vow. Jesus coming near to a dead body violates the vow of the Nazarite. Jesus actually touched a dead body when he raised a young girl to life.

Mark 5:40-41 And they laughed him to scorn. But when he had put them all out, he taketh the father and the mother of the damsel, and them that were with him, and entereth in where the damsel was lying. 41 And he took the damsel by the hand, and said unto her, Talitha cumi; which is, being interpreted, Damsel, I say unto thee, arise.

And even a liberal interpretation finds difficulty explaining why a Nazarite would make wine. A Nazarite making wine is parallel to explaining Samson in a vineyard.

John 2:7-9 Jesus saith unto them, Fill the waterpots with water. And they filled them up to the brim. 8 And he saith unto them, Draw out now, and bear unto the governor of the feast. And they bare it. 9 When the ruler of the feast had tasted the water that was made wine, and knew not whence it was: (but the servants which drew the water knew;) the governor of the feast called the bridegroom,

BLOOD

Just as God associates grapes with blood, blood is associated with life. Blood is actually equated with life.

Genesis 9:4 But flesh with the life thereof, which is the blood thereof, shall ye not eat.

Leviticus 17:11 *For the life of the flesh is in the blood: and I have given it to you upon the altar to make an atonement for your souls: for it is the blood that maketh an atonement for the soul.*

The first mention of blood concerns Abel's murder by his brother, Cain. Notice Abel's blood is in the ground. In other words- the blood is out of his body. And where there is no blood; there is no life.

Genesis 4:8-11 *And Cain talked with Abel his brother: and it came to pass, when they were in the field, that Cain rose up against Abel his brother, and slew him.* **9** *And the LORD said unto Cain, Where is Abel thy brother? And he said, I know not: Am I my brother's keeper?* **10** *And he said, What hast thou done? the voice of thy brother's blood crieth unto me from the ground.* **11** *And now art thou cursed from the earth, which hath opened her mouth to receive thy brother's blood from thy hand;*

In both the Old Testament and the New Testament, God forbids his people to eat blood. This is one law given even to Christians.

Genesis 9:3-4 *Every moving thing that liveth shall be meat for you; even as the green herb have I given you all things.* **4** *But flesh with the life thereof, which is the blood thereof, shall ye not eat.*

Acts 15:28-29 *For it seemed good to the Holy Ghost, and to us, to lay upon you no greater burden than these necessary things;* **29** *That ye abstain from meats offered to idols, and from blood, and from things strangled, and from fornication: from which if ye keep yourselves, ye shall do well. Fare ye well.*

Leviticus 17:11-12 *For the life of the flesh is in the blood: and I have given it to you upon the altar to make an atonement for your souls: for it is the blood that maketh an atonement for the soul.* **12** *Therefore I said unto the children of Israel, No soul of you shall eat blood, neither shall any stranger that sojourneth among you eat blood.*

Deuteronomy 12:23 *Only be sure that thou eat not the blood: for the blood is the life; and thou mayest not eat the life with the flesh.*

The life of the flesh being in the blood defines the moment of death. Have you ever heard about someone who supposedly died and then came back to life? Sometimes this happens on an operating table in a hospital. The doctors confirm death via their machines, the heart stops, breathing stops, even activity in the brain ceases to register. And then, miraculously, life returns. It's as if the person returned from the dead. But this cannot be, because the Bible tells us a person dies only once. (before judgment)

Hebrews 9:27 *And as it is appointed unto men once to die, but after this the judgment:*

The explanation for those who apparently die and then return to life is they were only clinically dead. Since life is in the blood, their blood still supported life. Once the oxygen is gone from the blood, however, or once the blood coagulates or is depleted, then a person is dead. And when that happens- there is no returning with a story to tell Reader's Digest or a television talk show.

Obviously blood has huge importance in a human body. Since blood is keeping our physical bodies alive. And since it is a fact our present flesh is corrupted or (fallen). A logical question is, did human beings have blood in them before the fall?

Blood was a consequence of the fall. Consider the following logic. We know the fall ultimately brought death to the human body. The human body is corruptible flesh. Blood keeps the human being's unregenerate, dying flesh alive.

Leviticus 17:11 *For the life of the flesh is in the blood: and I have given it to you upon the altar to make an atonement for your souls: for it is the blood that maketh an atonement for the soul.*

A Christian's body is not saved, or born again until the rapture.

Romans 8:10 *And if Christ be in you, the body is dead because of sin; but the Spirit is life because of righteousness.*

Presently, when a person gets saved, his/her soul is redeemed and granted eternal life, but this is only the first fruits of salvation. *Romans 8:23* -informs Christians they still wait for the body's redemption.

Romans 8:23 *And not only they, but ourselves also, which have the firstfruits of the Spirit, even we ourselves groan within ourselves, waiting for the adoption, to wit, the redemption of our body.*

Scripture declares a Christian's flesh corrupt and, therefore, it must change in order to get into heaven. Consider the state of flesh in its present condition- as opposed to the way we live in heaven. Although the passage below concerns the rapture, concentrate on what is physically happening to the flesh. It goes through a physical change. Why, because our present bodies could not stay alive in heaven. To live in heaven we need supernatural bodies. Just like a trip to the moon requires a space suit to stay alive- Your voyage to heaven requires a new body. That new body lives without blood. God tells us plainly that flesh and blood will not go to heaven.

1 Corinthians 15:50-54 *Now this I say, brethren, **that flesh and blood cannot inherit the kingdom of God**; neither doth corruption inherit incorruption. **51** Behold, I shew you a mystery; We shall not all sleep, but we shall all be changed, **52** In a moment, in the twinkling of an eye, at the last trump: for the trumpet shall sound, and the dead shall be raised incorruptible, and we shall be changed. **53** For this corruptible must put on incorruption, and this mortal must put on immortality. **54** So when this corruptible shall have put on incorruption, and this mortal shall have put on immortality, then shall be brought to pass the saying that is written, Death is swallowed up in victory.*

Notice the body or the flesh is changed from a corruptible state to an incorruptible state. But nothing was said about the blood changing. Our mortal bodies needed blood to stay alive; immortal bodies do not.

In heaven we are like Jesus, even to the point of having a body like his. Remember Jesus shed his blood before he went to heaven. After his resurrection, Jesus confronted the Apostles. Jesus told them to touch his body. Jesus said he was flesh and bone; He did not mention blood.

*Luke 24:36-40 And as they thus spake, Jesus himself stood in the midst of them, and saith unto them, Peace be unto you. **37** But they were terrified and affrighted, and supposed that they had seen a spirit. **38** And he said unto them, Why are ye troubled? and why do thoughts arise in your hearts? **39** Behold my hands and my feet, that it is I myself: handle me, and see; **for a spirit hath not flesh and bones,** as ye see me have. **40** And when he had thus spoken, he shewed them his hands and his feet.*

1 John 3:2 Beloved, now are we the sons of God, and it doth not yet appear what we shall be: but we know that, when he shall appear, we shall be like him; for we shall see him as he is.

WHAT HAPPENED TO HUMAN FLESH AT THE FALL?

Consider, for a moment, the bodies of Adam and Eve before the fall. Consider those bodies in the context of *1ˢᵗ Corinthians 15:51-54.* Not only Eden's environment was perfect, human bodies were perfect. No sickness, disease, or even aging (in the sense of decay). The fall brought death. The Garden of Eden, before the fall, was quite literally heaven on earth. Therefore, if flesh and blood cannot inherit heaven, then doesn't it make sense Adam and Eve (originally) lived in bodies like the ones Christians get at the rapture?

THE RAPTURE IN REVERSE

The fall changed Adam and Eve physically. What happened to Adam and Eve at the fall was the antithesis or the exact opposite of what happens to Christians at the rapture. It was the rapture in reverse. Adam and Eve's incorruptible body put on corruption. Immortality put on mortality. Life was swallowed up in defeat. Read the passage below and reverse what's happening to the physical body.

1 Corinthians 15:53-54 For this corruptible must put on incorruption, and this mortal must put on immortality. 54 So when this corruptible shall have put on incorruption, and this mortal shall have put on immortality, then shall be brought to pass the saying that is written, Death is swallowed up in victory.

Consider also the statement God makes about clothing Adam and Eve. Often Christians presume God killed a lamb and clothed Adam and Eve with the animal's skin; but, there is no mention of this in the Bible. I think it more likely that the *coats of skins* are the skin (flesh) people are in today? A consequence of the fall is mankind received their new, corruptible, fallen bodies? And after God made his children *coats of skin-* he then clothed them with a garment. That garment may or may not have been a lamb. A lamb actually fits typology quite well, but it is inferred; it is not scripture. *Read Genesis 3:21* slowly and carefully. Observe the comma.

Genesis 3:21 Unto Adam also and to his wife did the LORD God make coats of skins, and clothed them.

Now read Job's very interesting and illuminating commentary. Let the scripture define clothes. Job rehearses God's creation of man. In verse 11, **Job declares God clothed him with skin and flesh.**

*Job 10:8-11 Thine hands have made me and fashioned me together round about; yet thou dost destroy me. 9 Remember, I beseech thee, that thou hast made me as the clay; and wilt thou bring me into dust again? 10 Hast thou not poured me out as milk, and curdled me like cheese? 11 **Thou hast clothed me with skin and flesh,** and hast fenced me with bones and sinews.*

Based on biblical research, I am persuaded Adam and Eve did not have blood in them until they ate the forbidden fruit, which was indeed a grape. Bad blood defiled the original perfect flesh like a virus, transforming it into a corrupt and dying body. Every health problem human beings have -from common colds to cancer- from birth defects to aging is a blood problem. If doctors could fix the blood, they could cure any disease.

TREE OF KNOWLEDGE OF GOOD AND EVIL

In the Garden of Eden two trees were paramount, a tree of life and a tree of the knowledge of good and evil. This chapter focuses on the tree of knowledge of good and evil.

Adam and Noah are the two ultimate patriarchs when it comes to planet earth's human population. Both characters lived after cataclysmic floods. Both men sinned in a garden. It is these parallels together with other scriptural considerations (especially the Nazarite's vow) which identify the fruit from the tree of knowledge of good and evil as a grape. The charts below displays significant parallels between Noah and Adam.

LIFE CHART: ADAM AND NOAH

ADAM:

1. Main Character after a flood- Gen. 1:2
2. Receives Blessing- Gen. 1:28
3. Has 3 sons: Seth, Abel, Cain
4. **Sins in a Garden- Gen. 3:6**
5. One son sins Gen. 4:8
6. One son cursed- Cain Gen. 4:11
7. Son's genealogical line drawn to God.
   Seth - Noah

NOAH:

1. Main Character after a flood-Gen. 7:10
2. Receives Identical Blessing- Gen 9:1-3
3. Has 3 sons: Shem, Japheth, Ham
4. **Sins in a Garden-   Gen. 9:20-21**
5. One son sins Gen. 9:24
6. One son cursed- Canaan Gen. 9:25
7. Son's genealogical line drawn to God. Shem- Abraham

Aligning the chart's information with curious doctrinal criteria of the Nazarite's vow enables a Bible student to make an educated guess. Point number four in the chart, allows intelligent speculation that the fruit of the tree of knowledge of good and evil was a grape. Noah got drunk on wine-- and wine comes from grapes. Considering the consistent parallels of Adam's and Noah's lives, the fruit has been identified. While it is true grapes grow on a vine, the Bible defines the vine as a tree. The Bible interprets itself, further substantiating the fruit is a grape.

*Numbers 6:3-4 He shall separate himself from wine and strong drink, and shall drink no vinegar of wine, or vinegar of strong drink, neither shall he drink any liquor of grapes, nor eat moist grapes, or dried. 4 All the days of his separation shall he eat nothing that is **made of the vine tree,** from the kernels even to the husk.*

Knowing the tree of knowledge of good and evil was a vine tree explains the reasoning behind God forbidding Nazarites to eat grapes. God's memory holds the original act of Adam's fall. When a Jew takes the vow of a Nazarite, it symbolizes refusing to partake of the tree of knowledge of good and evil; therefore grapes are forbidden. Also noteworthy, a vine tree left unattended grows on the ground and looks like a serpent or a snake.

A word of caution- the Nazarite's vow was a voluntary, temporary submission to a lifestyle, with the goal of drawing oneself to God. Forbidding grapes in all forms today or viewing grapes as evil would be incorrect.

Genesis 3:6 And when the woman saw that the tree was good for food, and that it was pleasant to the eyes, and a tree to be desired to make one wise, she took of the fruit thereof, and did eat, and gave also unto her husband with her; and he did eat.

Genesis 9:20-21 And Noah began to be an husbandman, and he planted a vineyard: 21 And he drank of the wine, and was drunken; and he was uncovered within his tent.

King of Salem

GENESIS 14:18 *AND MELCHIZEDEK KING of Salem brought forth bread and wine: and he was the priest of the most high God.*

Introducing Melchizedek

§

HEBREWS **7:4** *NOW CONSIDER HOW great this man was, unto whom even the patriarch Abraham gave the tenth of the spoils.*

God commands believers to consider two men: Melchizedek and Jesus Christ. Melchizedek is priest of the most high God, yet his priesthood's doctrines remain undisclosed. Melchizedek is King of Salem, but Salem's residents dwell hidden and unknown. Scriptures declare no man righteous, yet Melchizedek is called King of righteousness. After considering Melchizedek for nearly four thousand years, the elusive king priest remains an enigma in God's eternal plan. God charges Christians to consider how great this man was, let us pray God show us how to learn. Grounded in biblical investigation, *Consider Melchizedek* provokes dialogue and thought.

Hebrews **5:10-11** *Called of God an high priest after the order of Melchisedec.* **11** *Of whom we have many things to say, and hard to be uttered, seeing ye are dull of hearing.*

Hebrews 5:10-11 remains fresh and accusing. The writers of Hebrews said many things about Melchizedek, yet he persists in mystery. Christianity's studied opinions basically narrow to four ideas. The author believes all four theories incorrect.

1. Melchizedek is pre-incarnate Jesus Christ.
2. Melchizedek is Shem- the son of Noah.
3. Melchizedek is an angel.
4. Melchizedek is unknowable.

Genesis 14:18-20 *And Melchizedek king of Salem brought forth bread and wine: and he was the priest of the most high God.* **19** *And he blessed him, and said, Blessed be Abram of the most high God, possessor of heaven and earth:* **20** *And blessed be the most high God, which hath delivered thine enemies into thy hand. And he gave him tithes of all.*

As Abram returns from a successful military operation undertaken to rescue his nephew, Lot, Melchizedek emerges onto human history. Melchizedek celebrates Abram's victory by blessing him and acknowledging God's intervention in the battle. Whether the two men knew each other or they meet here for the first time is unknown. Abram responds by tithing the spoils of war directly to Melchizedek. After the brief religious ceremony and prayer, Melchizedek departs from biblical record as mysteriously as he arrived. The Lord briefly mentions him again in *Psalm 110:4*

Psalms 110:4 *The LORD hath sworn, and will not repent, Thou art a priest for ever after the order of Melchizedek.*

Hebrews 7:4 *Now consider how great this man was, unto whom even the patriarch Abraham gave the tenth of the spoils.*

Scripture identifies Melchizedek as the first priest. Abraham's relationship with God did not require priesthood. Although the patriarchs participated in sacrificial offerings, God did not require an organized religious priesthood. Interestingly, Melchizedek's priesthood existed hundreds of years before the days of Aaron and the Levitical priesthood.

Salem

§

MELCHIZEDEK'S HOME, SALEM, APPEARS ONLY four times in the Bible. Since Melchizedek's titles include *priest of the most-high God*, we may infer Salem's residents worship God under Melchizedek's priestly order. Is Salem an entire kingdom or just a city, or perhaps a tribe? Many historians theorize Salem is Jerusalem; however, that hypothesis is presumptuous. Joab and King David conquer Jerusalem around 1,048 BC. Before then the Amorites and Jebusites controlled the city. When God announces Melchizedek King of Salem, it's around 1,910 BC- nearly 900 years before Israel owns Jerusalem. And considering Melchizedek's endless life, he certainly could have been king of Salem for much longer.

Definitions:

Salem: at peace, complete: perfect
Jerusalem: dual peace; lay (set) ye double peace
Melchizedek: King of righteousness

Observe the Bible interprets Salem as meaning peace. Salem's definition also includes perfection.

Hebrews 7:2 *To whom also Abraham gave a tenth part of all; first-being by interpretation King of righteousness, and after that also King of Salem, which is, King of peace;*

Psalms 76:1-3 *To the chief Musician on Neginoth, A Psalm or Song of Asaph. In Judah is God known: his name is great in Israel. 2 In Salem also is his tabernacle, and his dwelling place in Zion. 3 There brake he the arrows of the bow, the shield, and the sword, and the battle. Selah.*

Psalm 76 proclaims God's tabernacle is also in Salem; scripture using the word ***also*** is important. God refers not only to a physical tent like structure; but rather what the tabernacle represents, holy and true worship. (In much the same way, Christians use the word church) Thus I conclude proper and organized worship happened also in Salem as well as Jerusalem. When David references Salem, he is not saying Salem is Jerusalem. Indeed, Salem compares spiritually to Jerusalem, but it's another place entirely. Like Melchizedek, Salem is fraught with mystery.

Psalms 110:4 *The LORD hath sworn, and will not repent, Thou art a priest for ever after the order of Melchizedek.*

The Lord Jesus is a priest for ever after the order of Melchizedek. Curiously, God skips over Aaron (representing the Levitical priesthood).

THE CHRONOLOGICAL ORDER OF PRIESTHOODS:

1. Melchizedek
2. Aaron
3. Jesus Christ

Priest Melchizedek

§

*HEBREWS 5:1-6 FOR EVERY HIGH priest taken from among men is or-
dained for men in things pertaining to God, that he may offer both gifts
and sacrifices for sins: 2 Who can have compassion on the ignorant, and
on them that are out of the way; for that he himself also is compassed with
infirmity. 3 And by reason hereof he ought, as for the people, so also for
himself, to offer for sins. 4 And no man taketh this honour unto himself,
but he that is called of God, as was Aaron. 5 So also Christ glorified not
himself to be made an high priest; but he that said unto him, Thou art my
Son, to day have I begotten thee. 6 As he saith also in another place, Thou
art a priest for ever after the order of Melchisedec.*

Melchizedek's reference in verse 6 is remarkable. After reading
Hebrews 5:1-5, one expects God to say thou art a priest for ever after
the order of Aaron; because under Levitical Law, Aaron served as
the first high priest. But God does not say after Aaron; God says
after the order of Melchizedek. Just as in the Old Testament, God
skips over Aaron. God does not discuss the orders or doctrines of
Melchizedek's priesthood, not here anyway. God's high priests, representing their respective dispensations, running in chronological
order are: Melchizedek- Aaron- Jesus Christ.

*Hebrews 5:7-10 Who in the days of his flesh, when he had offered up
prayers and supplications with strong crying and tears unto him that was*

*able to save him from death, and was heard in that he feared; **8** Though he were a Son, yet learned he obedience by the things which he suffered; **9** And being made perfect, he became the author of eternal salvation unto all them that obey him; **10** Called of God an high priest after the order of Melchisedec.*

Verses 7-9 concern the Lord Jesus Christ, for Jesus, alone, is the author of eternal salvation. And then, in verse 10, God the Father ignores Aaron, and calls Jesus a high priest after the order of Melchizedek.

GOD'S PREPARATION FOR BELIEVERS LEARNING MELCHIZEDEK

*Hebrews 5:11-14 Of whom we have many things to say, and hard to be uttered, seeing ye are dull of hearing. **12** For when for the time ye ought to be teachers, ye have need that one teach you again which be the first principles of the oracles of God; and are become such as have need of milk, and not of strong meat. **13** For every one that useth milk is unskilful in the word of righteousness: for he is a babe. **14** But strong meat belongeth to them that are of full age, even those who by reason of use have their senses exercised to discern both good and evil.*

Verses 11-14 begins elaborating on Melchizedek. God knows serious readers focus on the continuing references to Melchizedek. Hebrews' writers have many things to say; but scripture implies most believers resist strong meat. Whatever God says about Melchizedek constitutes very mature doctrine. Since the study's focus is Melchizedek, let's begin in *Hebrews 6:13.*

*Hebrews 6:13-20 For when God made promise to Abraham, because he could swear by no greater, he sware by himself, **14** Saying, Surely blessing I will bless thee, and multiplying I will multiply thee. **15** And so, after he had patiently endured, he obtained the promise. **16** For men verily swear*

by the greater: and an oath for confirmation is to them an end of all strife.
17 Wherein God, willing more abundantly to shew unto the heirs of prom-
ise the immutability of his counsel, confirmed it by an oath: 18 That by two
immutable things, in which it was impossible for God to lie, we might have
a strong consolation, who have fled for refuge to lay hold upon the hope set
before us: 19 Which hope we have as an anchor of the soul, both sure and
stedfast, and which entereth into that within the veil; 20 Whither the fore-
runner is for us entered, even Jesus, made an high priest for ever after the
order of Melchisedec.

The above passage expounds the promise to Abraham. Very interesting because God moves historically backward in the narrative. God
discussed the Levitical priesthood in chapter 5, and now in chapter
6, he addresses the Abrahamic covenant. God concludes both passages with references to Melchizedek. Throughout chapters 5-7, God
divides categories of doctrinal thought by references to Melchizedek.

The historical regression means Melchizedek's priesthood precedes the Abrahamic covenant. This makes perfect sense because
Melchizedek already functions as a priest when Abraham meets him.
Hebrews 7:1-21 belongs to the King of Salem. The passage covers
material learned in *Genesis 14.* The verse also defines Salem as peace.

Hebrews 7:1-2 For this Melchisedec, king of Salem, priest of the most
high God, who met Abraham returning from the slaughter of the kings,
and blessed him; 2 To whom also Abraham gave a tenth part of all; first
being by interpretation King of righteousness, and after that also King of
Salem, which is, King of peace;

WITHOUT FATHER, WITHOUT MOTHER

Hebrews 7:3 Without father, without mother, without descent, having
neither beginning of days, nor end of life; but made like unto the Son of
*God; **abideth a priest continually***

Hebrews 7:3 convinces many that Melchizedek was a pre-incarnation of Jesus Christ, or an angel. But let's think through each descriptive element in the verse. The Scripture does not say Melchizedek never had parents; it says he is without them. A person can lose their parents in an accident and be without them. In other words his parents are dead. When Abraham met Melchizedek, he was without parents.

WITHOUT DESCENT

When scripture says Melchizedek is without descent, meaning God chooses to withhold his lineage. Compare the statement to *Hebrews 7:6*, where a descent is mentioned; it's just not counted from the Levites!

Hebrews 7:6 *But **he whose descent** is not counted from them received tithes of Abraham, and blessed him that had the promises.*

The statement **he whose descent** declares Melchizedek has a descent. The antecedent for the word *he-* is Melchizedek; the antecedent for the word *them* are the Levites. Melchizedek's descent is not counted from the Levites. God chooses not to give us his descent, because in the context of the dialogue, it would confuse the issue. Indeed, by withholding Melchizedek's descent, God makes him more important.

The passage provides evidence for Melchizedek not being Jesus, because Jesus has a legal descent recorded in scripture through the line of David. Jesus also has a Father and a mother.

HAVING NEITHER BEGINNING OF LIFE, NOR END OF LIFE

Without a recorded lineage, we do not know his beginning of life. This concerns the power of what God writes down. It also implies Melchizedek existed when the age of fallen mankind began. God states plainly Melchizedek never dies.

BUT MADE LIKE UNTO THE SON OF GOD

God makes Melchizedek like the Son of God. Melchizedek is like Jesus; but he is not Jesus. Imagine someone saying Jesus was only like (or similar to) God. Jesus Christ is God. Furthermore, if Melchizedek is Jesus, why does Scripture declare Jesus came after the order of Melchizedek?

ABIDETH A PRIEST CONTINUALLY

Observe also Melchizedek abides as priest continually, which means he is still serving as priest. Jesus served as priest and sat down. Abiding as a priest continually is truly a ponderous situation. God wrote Hebrews 2,000 years after introducing Melchizedek in the Old Testament. Melchizedek continues as a functioning priest even after the death and resurrection of Jesus Christ. Remember Melchizedek serves God in Salem.

CONSIDER MELCHIZEDEK

Hebrews 7:4-10 Now consider how great this man was, unto whom even the patriarch Abraham gave the tenth of the spoils. 5 And verily they that are of the sons of Levi, who receive the office of the priesthood, have a commandment to take tithes of the people according to the law, that is, of their brethren, though they come out of the loins of Abraham: 6 But he whose descent is not counted from them received tithes of Abraham, and blessed him that had the promises. 7 And without all contradiction the less is blessed of the better.

8 And here men that die receive tithes; but there he receiveth them, of whom it is witnessed that he liveth. 9 And as I may so say, Levi also, who receiveth tithes, payed tithes in Abraham. 10 For he was yet in the loins of his father, when Melchisedec met him.

Look carefully at verse 8:

here men receive tithes, **Where is here?**
but there he receiveth them, **Where is there?**

Summary of facts

1. Melchizedek has a descent; it's just not counted from Levites.
2. Melchizedek is better than Abraham.
3. Melchizedek lives forever.
4. Melchizedek abides as priest continually.
5. Levitical priesthood paid tithes to Melchizedek.

Melchizedek being better than Abraham is hugely important. There seems little room for doctrinal application *of Psalms 53, or Romans 2:11; 10:3-5 to* a man better than Abraham; a man God calls King of righteousness. Considering how great this man is, I conclude Melchizedek very different from fallen sons of Adam and Eve. And since Melchizedek serves as priest continually, who are the people still benefiting from his priesthood?

Hebrews 7:11-12 If therefore perfection were by the Levitical priesthood, (for under it the people received the law,) what further need was there that another priest should rise after the order of Melchisedec, and not be called after the order of Aaron? 12 For the priesthood being changed, there is made of necessity a change also of the law.

Hebrews 7:11- asks a question Christians can answer. We know perfection was not obtained under the Levitical priesthood. That's why Jesus came, died, and rose again. And those who come to Jesus are made perfect in Him. But look at this continued ignoring of the dispensation of the Law when Melchizedek is around. God discusses the Levitical priesthood as a parenthetical insert between Melchizedek and Jesus Christ.

It looks to me like Melchizedek's priestly order is perfect, but for some reason, Melchizedek's priesthood cannot benefit Abraham's descendants, but why? Why couldn't Melchizedek's continuing priesthood suffice for Israel?

ANOTHER TRIBE

*Hebrews 7:12-17 For the priesthood being changed, there is made of necessity a change also of the law. **13 For he of whom these things are spoken pertaineth to another tribe, of which no man gave attendance at the altar. 14 For it is evident that our Lord sprang out of Juda; of which** tribe Moses spake nothing concerning priesthood. **15 And it is yet far more** evident: for that after the similitude of Melchisedec there ariseth another priest, **16** Who is made, not after the law of a carnal commandment, but after the power of an endless life. **17** For he testifieth, Thou art a priest for ever after the order of Melchisedec.*

Look carefully at verse 13. Who is God talking about here, Jesus or Melchizedek? Is the *another tribe* Judah, or some unnamed tribe? I suggest that God speaks of Melchizedek and the tribe is not Judah; the tribe remains unnamed (in the passage)

DON'T CONFUSE THE ALTAR WITH THE MOST HOLY PLACE OR THE ARK OF THE COVENANT.

To correctly identify this tribe- it must be a tribe which no man gave attendance at the altar. It is true only the Levite high priest stood before the ark in the temple's most holy place, but elders from all Israel's 12 tribes stood before the brazen altar. Being in attendance is quite different than serving as high priest.

Numbers 7:10-11 And the princes offered for dedicating of the altar in the day that it was anointed, even the princes offered their offering before the altar. **11** *And the LORD said unto Moses, They shall offer their offering, each prince on his day, for the dedicating of the altar.*

King David even made offerings before the Ark wearing an ephod; therefore, the other tribe cannot be Judah. It is Melchizedek's tribe that no man represented at the altar. Melchizedek is king of Salem; the other tribe is Salem. This is fascinating because it means God considers Melchizedek's people a tribe of Israel. God associates the word tribe exclusively with Israel. God calls Gentile peoples nations, countries, and kingdoms.

Jesus compares to the similitude of Melchizedek because God never subjected Melchizedek to the Levitical order. Melchizedek enjoys endless life. Jesus, obviously, has eternal life for He is the great I AM; therefore, Jesus has far more in common with Melchizedek the King of righteousness, than He does with any Levitical high priest.

If human beings had a perfect priesthood under the order of Melchizedek, why did God set up the Levitical priesthood? Answer: Because Melchizedek remains a priest for a different kind of people; suppose God has a people not related to a fallen Adam and Eve.

2 Samuel 6:14-18 *And David danced before the LORD with all his might; and David was girded with a linen ephod.* **15** *So David and all the house of Israel brought up the ark of the LORD with shouting, and with the sound of the trumpet.* **16** *And as the ark of the LORD came into the city of David, Michal Saul's daughter looked through a window, and saw king David leaping and dancing before the LORD; and she despised him in her heart.* **17** *And they brought in the ark of the LORD, and set it in his place, in the midst of the tabernacle that David had pitched for it: and David offered burnt offerings and peace offerings before the LORD.* **18** *And as soon as David had made an end of offering burnt offerings and peace offerings, he blessed the people in the name of the LORD of hosts.*

Leviticus 4:14-18 *When the sin, which they have sinned against it, is known, then the congregation shall offer a young bullock for the sin, and* *bring him before the tabernacle of the congregation.* **15** ***And the elders of the congregation shall lay their hands upon the head of the bullock before the LORD:*** *and the bullock shall be killed before the LORD.* **16** *And the priest that is anointed shall bring of the bullock's blood to the tabernacle of the congregation:*

Melchizedek's Origin

§

HYPOTHESIS:

MELCHIZEDEK IS A SON OF Adam and Eve; likely their first born. He lived before Adam and Eve ate from the tree of knowledge of good and evil; therefore Melchizedek does not have a corrupt Adamic nature. God separated him from the fallen sons of Adam. Melchizedek ate from the tree of life and will never die.

SEPARATED SONS OF ADAM LINKED TO ISRAEL:

Deuteronomy 32:7-8 Remember the days of old, consider the years of many generations: ask thy father, and he will shew thee; thy elders, and they will tell thee. 8 When the most High divided to the nations their inheritance, when he separated the sons of Adam, he set the bounds of the people according to the number of the children of Israel.

EVIDENCE

Did you ever notice when Adam called Eve the *mother of all living* -Cain and Abel had not yet been born? Why would Adam call Eve the mother of all living if she hadn't birthed any children?

Genesis 3:20 *And Adam called his wife's name Eve; because she was the mother of all living.*

Cain and Able are not born until Genesis 4:1-2

Genesis 4:1-2 *And Adam knew Eve his wife; and she conceived, and bare Cain, and said, I have gotten a man from the LORD. 2 And she again bare his brother Abel. And Abel was a keeper of sheep, but Cain was a tiller of the ground.*

Persons insisting Cain and Abel are Adam's and Eve's first children assert *Genesis 3:20-* is historically parenthetical. In other words- God puts the verse chronologically out of order with the rest of the chapter. Such reasoning disrupts the passage's historical integrity. Read carefully Genesis chapter 3. Every verse in chapter 3 seems in exact chronological order. The doctrine of Adam and Eve not having children until chapter 4, is believed (by most Christians) without question, without thinking, and without investigation. God put the verse where he did for a reason.

Examining the Curse

§

Perhaps the strongest evidence for Adam and Eve having children before the Fall is the examination of God's curse. Compare the way things were before the Fall to the way things are after the Fall.

Genesis 3:14-20 And the LORD God said unto the serpent, Because thou hast done this, thou art cursed above all cattle, and above every beast of the field; upon thy belly shalt thou go, and dust shalt thou eat all the days of thy life: 15 And I will put enmity between thee and the woman, and between thy seed and her seed; it shall bruise thy head, and thou shalt bruise his heel. 16 Unto the woman he said, I will greatly multiply thy sorrow and thy conception; in sorrow thou shalt bring forth children; and thy desire shall be to thy husband, and he shall rule over thee. 17 And unto Adam he said, Because thou hast hearkened unto the voice of thy wife, and hast eaten of the tree, of which I commanded thee, saying, Thou shalt not eat of it: cursed is the ground for thy sake; in sorrow shalt thou eat of it all the days of thy life; 18 Thorns also and thistles shall it bring forth to thee; and thou shalt eat the herb of the field; 19 In the sweat of thy face shalt thou eat bread, till thou return unto the ground; for out of it wast thou taken: for dust thou art, and unto dust shalt thou return. 20 And Adam called his wife's name Eve; because she was the mother of all living.

The above passage records God's response to the eating of the tree of knowledge of good and evil. Read very carefully the consequences delivered to God's creatures. Consider actions inflicted upon the serpent, the woman, Adam, and the earth. Notice the object cursed is rendered different than the way it was before the curse. Observe the creature's original state is physically changed.

God alters the original state of the serpent making him crawl upon his belly (and now he eats dust). Originally, the earth existed free from thorns and thistles. After the curse the earth grows them in abundance. Originally, Adam tended the garden with blessed joy and ease. After the curse, he must sweat and work for food.

Eve's punishment includes conception, child bearing. She originally produces children without sorrow. Now she delivers children with sorrow. If we conclude Eve did not have children before the Fall, we do not allow for a previous existence of curse free conception. Eve's conception and sorrow being multiplied is juxtaposed against her original state. How could her conception and sorrow be multiplied, if she never had children? Multiplied sorrow compared to what? As we interpret the curse for Adam, the earth, and the serpent- so must we do for Eve.

WHEN DID INNOCENCE END?

How long were Adam and Eve in Garden before they fell? The answer to this question is Adam's age of accountability. This study seeks to establish an educated guess on how long Adam and Eve lived in innocence. My purpose does not argue for an age of accountability in our present dispensation of grace; although, one should consider a spiritual application.

Hypothesis

Adam and Eve lived in the Garden of Eden in a state of innocence for twenty years. During their 20th year they ate from the tree of knowledge of good and evil. God held them accountable at age twenty- setting a precedent for responsible adulthood.

Strong correlations exist between the knowledge of good and evil, and God holding a person responsible for sin at twenty years old. God expounds the *knowledge of good and evil* 3 times. Examining these texts illuminates accountability. God's first references to the knowledge of good and evil concerns the creation of the tree in the Garden of Eden. One of the consequences from eating from the tree of knowledge of good and evil delivers humans the acquisition of knowledge. With the knowledge of good and evil acquired, God held Adam and Eve accountable. Prior to possessing this knowledge- God considered them innocent (or at least did not impute their sin.)

Genesis 2:8-9 And the LORD God planted a garden eastward in Eden; and there he put the man whom he had formed. 9 And out of the ground made the LORD God to grow every tree that is pleasant to the sight, and good for food; the tree of life also in the midst of the garden, and the tree of knowledge of good and evil.

Genesis 2:16-17 And the LORD God commanded the man, saying, Of every tree of the garden thou mayest freely eat: 17 But of the tree of the knowledge of good and evil, thou shalt not eat of it: for in the day that thou eatest thereof thou shalt surely die.

THE FALL of MAN

Genesis 3:6 And when the woman saw that the tree was good for food, and that it was pleasant to the eyes, and a tree to be desired to make one wise, she took of the fruit thereof, and did eat, and gave also unto her husband with her; and he did eat.

The Consequence: Accountability

Genesis 3:22 And the LORD God said, Behold, the man is become as one of us, to know good and evil: and now, lest he put forth his hand, and take also of the tree of life, and eat, and live for ever:

Nearly 2,500 years later, the words *knowledge of good and evil* appear again. God judges the entire nation of Israel according to their knowledge of good and evil. The reader should ponder events recorded in *Numbers chapters 13-15*. Additional pertinent information is discussed in *Deuteronomy 1and 2*. This study provides highlights and a summary of events from those chapters.

God passes judgment on Israel in the wilderness. But he exempts all persons under 20 because they had no knowledge between good and evil.

Summary of events:

As recorded in Exodus, Moses leads Israel out of oppressive Egyptian slavery, and the nation sets off toward the Promised Land. After spending a little more than one year in the wilderness, Moses sends twelve men to spy out the Promised Land. When those men return, only Joshua and Caleb offer a positive view of the land. The other ten men tell of giants and convince Israel the people beyond the Jordan are too powerful to defeat in battle. The negative report discourages Israel and they refuse to possess the land. In disobedience to God, the majority argues for Israel's return to Egypt.

Numbers 14:2-4 And all the children of Israel murmured against Moses and against Aaron: and the whole congregation said unto them, Would God that we had died in the land of Egypt! or would God we had died in this wilderness! 3 And wherefore hath the LORD brought us unto this land, to fall by the sword, that our wives and our children should be a prey? were it not better for us to return into Egypt? 4 And they said one to another, Let us make a captain, and let us return into Egypt.

The whole episode infuriates the Lord, and he passes judgment on the entire nation. **This judgment merits a Christian's utmost scrutiny.** God did not hold people under twenty years old accountable. God declares persons under twenty years old had no knowledge between good and evil, therefore, he exempted them from full consequences of judgment. Persons twenty years old and above were held accountable.

Numbers 14:27-35 *How long shall I bear with this evil congregation, which murmur against me? I have heard the murmurings of the children of Israel, which they murmur against me. 28 Say unto them, As truly as I live, saith the LORD, as ye have spoken in mine ears, so will I do to you: 29* ***Your carcases shall fall in this wilderness; and all that were numbered of you, according to your whole number, from twenty years old and upward, which have murmured against me, 30*** *Doubtless ye shall not come into the land, concerning which I sware to make you dwell therein, save Caleb the son of Jephunneh, and Joshua the son of Nun. 31* ***But your little ones, which ye said should be a prey, them will I bring in, and they shall know the land which ye have despised. 32 But as for you, your carcases, they shall fall in this wilderness. 33*** *And your children shall wander in the wilderness forty years, and bear your whoredoms, until your carcases be wasted in the wilderness. 34 After the number of the days in which ye searched the land, even forty days, each day for a year, shall ye bear your iniquities, even forty years, and ye shall know my breach of promise. 35 I the LORD have said, I will surely do it unto all this evil congregation, that are gathered together against me: in this wilderness they shall be consumed, and there they shall die.*

Deuteronomy 1:39 *Moreover your little ones, which ye said should be a prey, and your children,* **which in that day had no knowledge between good and evil,** *they shall go in thither, and unto them will I give it, and they shall possess it.*

Numbers 32:11 Surely none of the men that came up out of Egypt, from twenty years old and upward, shall see the land *which I sware unto Abraham, unto Isaac, and unto Jacob; because they have not wholly followed me:*

Think about this declaration. A twenty year old and a nineteen year old both murmur against Moses and both disobey the Lord. But when God delivers judgment, only the twenty year old is held responsible for his sin. Sin is not imputed to any Israelite under twenty! God draws a clear line; in this particular instance-twenty years old is the age of accountability. As we shall see, however, this is not the only time God designates twenty years old as the age for maturity and responsibility.

ATONEMENT FOR A SOUL

Even before the Jews refused to take the Promised Land, God established the age of twenty legally important. In the passage below God teaches a critical doctrine. The amount of money is not the focus; all souls are equally valued. But God mandates children less than twenty years old do not require a ransom or payment. God exempted people under twenty from making an atonement offering for their souls.

Exodus 30:11-15 *And the LORD spake unto Moses, saying,* ***12*** *When thou takest the sum of the children of Israel after their number, then shall they give every man a ransom for his soul unto the LORD, when thou numberest them; that there be no plague among them, when thou number-est them.* ***13*** *This they shall give, every one that passeth among them that are numbered, half a shekel after the shekel of the sanctuary: (a shekel is twenty gerahs:) an half shekel shall be the offering of the LORD.* ***14*** *Every one that passeth among them that are numbered, from twenty years old and above, shall give an offering unto the LORD.* ***15*** *The rich shall not give* *more, and the poor shall not give less than half a shekel, when they give an offering unto the LORD, to make an atonement for your souls.*

Over and over again, the Bible designates age twenty as the age God considers people accountable for their actions. When it came to counting people for war, for service in the priesthood, or for taking a census, the age twenty is consistent.

ADULT AGE FOR MILITARY SERVICE

Numbers 1:2-3 *Take ye the sum of all the congregation of the children of Israel, after their families, by the house of their fathers, with the number of their names, every male by their polls;* ***3*** *From twenty years old and upward, all that are able to go forth to war in Israel: thou and Aaron shall number them by their armies.*

Numbers 1:18-19 *And they assembled all the congregation together on the first day of the second month, and they declared their pedigrees after their families, by the house of their fathers, according to the number of the names, from twenty years old and upward, by their polls.* ***19*** *As the LORD commanded Moses, so he numbered them in the wilderness of Sinai.*

Numbers 26:1-2 *And it came to pass after the plague, that the LORD spake unto Moses and unto Eleazar the son of Aaron the priest, saying,* ***2*** *Take the sum of all the congregation of the children of Israel, from twenty years old and upward, throughout their fathers' house, all that are able to go to war in Israel.*

ADULT SERVICE FOR THE LORD

1 Chronicles 23:24 *These were the sons of Levi after the house of their fathers; even the chief of the fathers, as they were counted by number of names by their polls, that did the work for the service of the house of the LORD, from the age of twenty years and upward.*

Ezra 3:8 Now in the second year of their coming unto the house of God at Jerusalem, in the second month, began Zerubbabel the son of Shealtiel, and Jeshua the son of Jozadak, and the remnant of their brethren the priests and the Levites, and all they that were come out of the captivity unto Jerusalem; and appointed the Levites, from twenty years old and upward, to set forward the work of the house of the LORD.

GOOD AND EVIL IN THE NEW TESTAMENT

As learned, the term *knowledge of good and evil* correlates directly with accountability and responsibility for sin. The exact term *good and evil* appears only one time in the New Testament. Curiously, but not coincidently, *good and evil* appears in the same passage which introduces Melchizedek.

Hebrews 5:14 But strong meat belongeth to them that are of full age, even those who by reason of use have their senses exercised to discern both good and evil.

CLOSING THOUGHTS, QUESTIONS, THEORY

No matter how long Adam and Eve lived in the Garden of Eden, they obviously existed for some period of time. Does it matter? Consider: On the sixth day of creation, God creates the animal kingdom, as well as Adam and Eve. The same day God creates them, he commands reproduction.

Genesis 1:28 And God blessed them, and God said unto them, Be fruitful, and multiply, and replenish the earth, and subdue it: and have dominion over the fish of the sea, and over the fowl of the air, and over every living thing that moveth upon the earth.

For sake of dialogue, let's presume Adam and Eve did not reproduce before they ate the forbidden fruit. But what about the animal kingdom: the fish, birds, and land animals- did they reproduce? Would that matter?

After God commanded his creatures to be fruitful and multiply; how long do you think it took females of any species to be pregnant? Wouldn't a reasonable hypothesis conclude reproduction began immediately? And since God's response to the Fall invoked catastrophic consequences on the earth, man, and vegetation, wouldn't animals reproducing prior to the Fall have physiological and spiritual differences?

Just being obedient to God, Eve would be with child very soon after God introduced her to Adam. In fact, if one believes Cain and Abel are the first children, then one must theorize the Fall happened almost immediately.

Summary hypothesis

Adam (and Eve) beget Melchizedek before they disobeyed God; they produced other children also, at least one female. Her name is not given, but the Bible records none of the sister wives of the first generation. Obviously first generations married brothers and sisters; incest was not forbidden until *Leviticus 18*. Melchizedek is probably the eldest child, making him the patriarch of an unfallen race of human beings. He has everlasting spiritual life because he believed and obeyed God in not eating from the tree of knowledge of good and evil. And he has everlasting physical life because he ate from the tree of life in the Garden of Eden.

In order to protect the Garden of Eden and its unfallen inhabitants, God segregated and preserved it inside the earth. Paradise and Abraham's Bosom are synonymous with the Garden of Eden. Salem is another name for the tribe or entire region. Residents of Paradise are not held captive; only fallen children of Adam and Eve are forbidden access.

UNDER THE EARTH

The idea of people living under the earth may seem more like science fiction than a topic for Bible study. But God says plainly life inside the earth exists. Certainly hell's occupants are under the earth. But more things live under the earth than damned human souls. Examining the verses below leaves no doubt –Some kind of beings who love God live under the earth. This does not mean they would be trapped there; Melchizedek in Genesis 14 proves, the surface world is accessible, but Salem remains hidden to fallen human beings.

One could, perhaps, limit *Philippians 2:10* -to include only the damned souls under the earth. But *Rev. 5:3 and 5:13* are concerned with people who love God.

Philippians 2:10 *That at the name of Jesus every knee should bow, of things in heaven, and things in earth, and things under the earth;*

Revelation 5:3-4 *And no man in heaven, nor in earth, neither under the earth, was able to open the book, neither to look thereon. **4** And I wept much, because no man was found worthy to open and to read the book, neither to look thereon.*

Revelation 5:13 *And every creature which is in heaven, and on the earth, and under the earth, and such as are in the sea, and all that are in them, heard I saying, Blessing, and honour, and glory, and power, be unto him that sitteth upon the throne, and unto the Lamb for ever and ever.*

MANY MADE SINNERS

Romans 5:15 *But not as the offence, so also is the free gift. For if through the offence of one many be dead, much more the grace of God, and the gift by grace, which is by one man, Jesus Christ, hath abounded unto many.*

Romans 5:19 *For as by one man's disobedience many were made sinners, so by the obedience of one shall many be made righteous.*

Scripture directly juxtaposes Adam's disobedience to Jesus' obedience. Why doesn't God say all men instead of saying *many*? Only many persons are made righteous by Jesus' obedience because not all men believe in Jesus Christ. But why does God say many (instead of all) when discussing Adam's disobedience? Could it be because those born before the Fall did not disobey; therefore they were not made sinners?

But what about:

Romans 5:12-14 Wherefore, as by one man sin entered into the world, and death by sin; and so death passed upon all men, for that all have sinned: 13 (For until the law sin was in the world: but sin is not imputed when there is no law. 14 Nevertheless death reigned from Adam to Moses, even over them that had not sinned after the similitude of Adam's transgression, who is the figure of him that was to come.

Romans 5:12 says death passed upon all men. This is true, but the passage references Adam's lost world, mankind in fallen Adam? Death passing unto all men references those born after the Fall. God made Adam in his own image, but when Adam lost God's image, children were brought forth in Adam's fallen image. Adam lived in two worlds (or ages) a world before the Fall and a world after the Fall.

Genesis 5:3 And Adam lived an hundred and thirty years, and begat a son in his own likeness, after his image; and called his name Seth:

1 Corinthians 15:22 For as in Adam all die, even so in Christ shall all be made alive.

Here again the word all is used, but the *all* -represents a specific group. All men in Christ shall live. Likewise, human beings connected spiritually and physically to fallen Adam -die. If Adam begat children before he disobeyed God, they would not be in Adam. An unfallen Adam is an entirely different creature than a fallen Adam. And the text is speaking of fallen Adam. In a similar way, all men are not in Christ. A Christian is an entirely different being than a lost person. As the Bible student knows, all doctrinal truths do not apply to all dispensations.

THOUGHTS TO PONDER

God grants Christians eternal life the instant they are born again; their physical bodies given immortality at the Rapture. In the future, beyond the Rapture, Israelites and gentiles believe on Jesus Christ, but they must eat from the tree of life to gain physical immortality.

GAP

§

INTRODUCTION

IS THE EARTH ONLY 6,000 years old, or could it be much older? The Gap deals with a controversial Bible doctrine referred to as the gap theory. The idea God created heaven and earth in verse 1, and then destroyed it all in verse 2- is a subject of much debate. If the gap theory is correct, it essentially means an indeterminate span of time (or gap) exist in-between *Genesis 1:1 and Genesis 1:2*. And then God recreated the universe in six days as recorded in the remaining verses of the chapter. There is an opposing point of view to the gap. Many Christians believe God did not cancel his original creation, and no elapse of time between *Genesis 1:1 and Genesis 1:2* transpired. This Bible study's purpose is to present scriptural evidence supporting the gap did indeed happen. Although this is an extremely interesting and important subject, it should not become a test of fellowship. The Judgment seat of Christ will, no doubt, settle who's right and who's wrong on several issues.

2 Peter 3:5-7 For this they willingly are ignorant of, that by the word of God the heavens were of old, and the earth standing out of the water and in the water: 6 Whereby the world that then was, being overflowed with water, perished: 7 But the heavens and the earth, which are now, by the same word are kept in store, reserved unto fire against the day of judgment and perdition of ungodly men.

Psalms 104:5-6 *Who laid the foundations of the earth, that it should not be removed for ever. 6 Thou coveredst it with the deep as with a garment: the waters stood above the mountains.*

Job 22:15-16 *Hast thou marked the old way which wicked men have trodden? 16 Which were cut down out of time, whose foundation was overflown with a flood:*

GAP

§

Genesis 1:1 In the beginning God created the heaven and the earth.

Genesis 1:2 And the earth was without form, and void; and darkness was upon the face of the deep. And the Spirit of God moved upon the face of the waters.

God created the heaven and the earth; then God made the earth without form and void. He also filled the heaven with a universe size body of water identified as the deep. The unknown span of time between *Genesis 1:1 and Genesis 1:2* is theologically, referred to as the *gap theory*. There is, however, no theory about it- the gap is there. This Bible study's purpose is to present scriptural evidence supporting the doctrine that an elapse of time exists between *Genesis 1:1 and Genesis 1:2*; consequently *Genesis.1:3-31* is an accounting of God recreating the universe.

In opposition to the Gap, many Christians believe God did not cancel or obliterate his original creation, and no elapse of time between *Genesis 1:1 and Genesis 1:2* even happened. They believe the earth is approximately 6,000 years old. Proponents of this theory are sometimes called the young earth theorists or creationists.

Perhaps the main argument set forth by young earth theorists asserts Christians believing the Gap compromised with evolution. Their point being- secular science teaches the earth is millions of years old, and a gap could agree with an evolutionary time line; therefore, Christians imagined the gap theory to agree with science. They suppose Christians were just too ignorant to defend the Bible against secular science and the evolutionists. But Christians holding to the gap fact believe emphatically in divine creation and stand opposed to evolution. Persons who think the gap agrees with evolution do not (or will not) comprehend the full teachings of the gap fact position.

Certainly Christians sometimes must agree to disagree, but let's be honest and clear about those differences of opinions. Christians who believe God voided his first creation also believe God created the moon, sun, and all the stars on the 4th day of the creation week, only about 6,000 years ago. Gap fact proponents believe only the earth is older. They also believe God created the first human beings, Adam and Eve, on the 6th day, approximately 6,000 years ago. Such beliefs provide no compromise with evolutionary science. Creationists know this, but they choose not to mention it as they try to defend their position by diminishing those who disagree with them. The very name "creationists" is misleading as it implies their view alone believes in divine creation.

Creationists primarily focus on when God made the earth. And anyone who disagrees with their interpretation supposedly compromises with evolution. Ironically, creationists constantly appeal to physical science to validate their interpretation of creation. In fact, many creationists seem more interested in fossil records and geography than they do in comparing scripture with scripture.

Another question young earth theorists ask is: When did this theological idea of the gap even come about? Thereby insinuating their position has been established doctrine for thousands of years. I propose an equally important question asks, when did the young earth theory come about?

Counting Backward

§

BEFORE DOING A VERSE BY verse account of *Genesis 1*, a summary of God's creation week reveals important information. To make this point more vivid, let's move backward starting with day seven and review what God created or accomplished on each specific day.

1. Day 7-God rests from his labor-Ge. 2:2
2. Day 6-Animals, Man -Ge. 1:24-31
3. Day 5-Aquatic life, birds- Ge. 20-23
4. Day 4-Sun, Moon, Stars- Ge. 1:14-19
5. Day 3-Gathers waters, land appears- Ge. 1:9-13
6. Day 2-Divides waters, firmament- Ge. 1:6-8
7. Day 1-Light- Ge. 1:3-5

Notice God did not create the earth during the creation week. God did not create the earth on the 4th day when he created the sun, moon, and the stars. The earth was already in existence. So even if someone does not believe in the gap, one must admit the earth is older than everything else in the universe, even if it's only a few days. Why do you suppose God does not record what day he made the earth?

The earth, made in verse 1, is not part of the creation week. God makes the earth void in verse 2. On day 3 God gathered the waters covering the earth into one place making the dry land appear, thus the earth already existed- although it had been submerged in water.

Void

§

GENESIS 1:1 IN THE BEGINNING God created the heaven and the earth.

Notice the singular heaven. In the beginning there were not three heavens as there are now. Originally, God created one uninterrupted infinite expanse of space.

Genesis 1:2 And the earth was without form, and void; and darkness was upon the face of the deep. And the Spirit of God moved upon the face of the waters.

Verse 2 declares the earth was without form and void. The first and primary definition of the word *void-* in English dictionaries means to cancel out, make invalid, or annul. A secondary definition defines *void* as empty or without. Comparing scripture with scripture, let's examine the way God uses the word *void*. The next three times God uses the word *void* it means to cancel or nullify. Consider the very next usage of the word *void* in *Numbers 30*. The scripture discusses a woman making a vow. If her husband so determine, **he can make void her vow**. In other words, he can cancel it.

Numbers 30:10-13 And if she vowed in her husband's house, or bound her soul by a bond with an oath; 11 And her husband heard it, and held his peace at her, and disallowed her not: then all her vows shall stand, and every bond wherewith she bound her soul shall stand. 12 But if her

husband hath utterly made them void on the day he heard them;
then whatsoever proceeded out of her lips concerning her vows, or
concerning the bond of her soul, shall not stand: her husband hath
made them void; and the LORD shall forgive her. 13 Every vow,
and every binding oath to afflict the soul, her husband may estab-
lish it, or her husband may make it void.

Even in today's modern times, if something corrupts an original check or a financial document, the bank recommends to write
VOID on it. And then write out a new document. The original, is
replaced with a new.

In the Bible, several places God uses the word *void* in the secondary definition- meaning without or empty. But it is not the first
or primary use of the word. **For sake of argument only-** Even
if one believes God uses the word *void* in the sense of being *empty*
or without --wouldn't it still look like something happened to the
earth after God created it?

After God created the heaven and the earth, he made it void. And
he filled the heaven with water. This water is called the deep. God
voided his creation by filling the universe with water- literally the
universe is flooded with water. Noah's flood, compared to this flood,
was minuscule. Noah's flood was only global. Why God obliterated
his initial creation is not revealed in this chapter, but something happened that provoked God's judgment. The Lucifer/ angelic rebellion
is a logical and educated guess.

***Genesis 1:3-8** And God said, Let there be light: and there was light. 4*
And God saw the light, that it was good: and God divided the light from the
darkness. 5 And God called the light Day, and the darkness he called Night.
And the evening and the morning were the first day. 6 And God said, Let
there be a firmament in the midst of the waters, and let it divide the waters
from the waters. 7 And God made the firmament, and divided the waters
which were under the firmament from the waters which were above the

firmament: and it was so. 8 And God called the firmament Heaven. And the evening and the morning were the second day.

As God pulls back the waters, the firmament appears. God calls the firmament heaven. Observe God creates the earth even before light! As of the 2nd day, the earth exists alone inside the firmament. This is a very important point: no record of the earth being created during the creation week; God creates the earth in verse one.

The Deep

§

GENESIS 1:2 AND THE EARTH was without form, and void; and darkness was upon the face of the deep. And the Spirit of God moved upon the face of the waters.

Genesis 1:7 And God made the firmament, and divided the waters which were under the firmament from the waters which were above the firmament: and it was so.

As God pulled back the waters, the firmament appeared. The cosmos being divided into three heavens is a consequence of the way God re-makes his universe. Inside the 1st heaven is the earth. Where earth's atmosphere ends, the 2nd heaven begins. The 2nd heaven contains the moon, sun, stars, and galaxies; it is literally outer space. At the end of the 2nd heaven is the deep, a body of water with enough volume to fill the 1st and 2nd heavens. The deep is a barrier separating the 2nd and the 3rd heaven. The 3rd heaven is infinite; it is where the city on sides of the North, God's temple, and God's Throne are located.

Read *Genesis 1:2-7* while considering the following analogy:

Imagine a basketball submerged deep into the ocean. Miles of water surround the ball on every side. Now imagine the basketball has infinite elasticity, and God begins pumping air into the ball. As the basketball enlarges it separates (pushes back) the deep water on every side. When the expansion stops the water remains above the rim of the basketball. The space inside the basketball is the firmament (heaven). And in this space God puts the stars, planets, sun, and the moon.

VERSES DEPICTING THREE HEAVENS: AND THE WATER BETWEEN THE 2ND AND 3RD HEAVEN:

Psalms 148:1-4 Praise ye the LORD. Praise ye the LORD from the heavens: praise him in the heights. 2 Praise ye him, all his angels: praise ye him, all his hosts. **3 Praise ye him, sun and moon: praise him, all ye stars of light. 4 Praise him, ye heavens of heavens, and ye waters that be above the heavens.**

2 Corinthians 12:2 I knew a man in Christ above fourteen years ago, (whether in the body, I cannot tell; or whether out of the body, I cannot tell: God knoweth;) such an one caught up to the third heaven.

1 Kings 8:27 But will God indeed dwell on the earth? behold, the heaven and heaven of heavens cannot contain thee; how much less this house that I have builded?

Psalms 11:4 The LORD is in his holy temple, the LORD'S throne is in heaven: his eyes behold, his eyelids try, the children of men.

Revelation 14:17 And another angel came out of the temple which is in heaven, he also having a sharp sickle.

In the future, after the Great White Throne Judgment- God re-creates the firmament. Notice God says there will be no more sea. The sea in *Re.21:1* is the deep. God returns the universe to its original design, one infinite expanse of heaven without the segregated barrier of the deep. In this passage, God refers to the deep as the sea. Presently, God views the earth from his throne in the 3rd heaven.

Inhabitants of the earth are quite literally underwater. Hence, the concept of being *fishers of men* has profound symbolic truth.

Revelation 21:1 *And I saw a new heaven and a new earth: for the first heaven and the first earth were passed away; and there was no more sea.*

Universal Flood

GENESIS 1:2 *AND THE EARTH was without form, and void; and darkness was upon the face of the deep. And the Spirit of God moved upon the face of the waters.*

    *2 **Peter** 3:5-7 For this they willingly are ignorant of, that by the word of God the heavens were of old, and the earth standing out of the water and in the water: **6** Whereby the world that then was, being overflowed with water, perished: **7 But the heavens and the earth, which are now,** by the same word are kept in store, reserved unto fire against the day of judgment and perdition of ungodly men.*

    2 Peter 3:5-7 is directed at the universal flood (as opposed to Noah's global flood) for the following reasons:

    But the heavens and the earth, which are now... Implicit in Peter's text is the understanding that today's heavens and the earth are different than they were in the past. Peter describes a flood which altered, if not obliterated the universe. We know this from God creating stars on the 4th day. In Noah's global flood, only the earth perished. In contrast, everything on the surface of the earth; and the entire preadamite world was made void. Nothing happened to the stars or the second heaven. Noah gazed into the same heavens and saw the same constellations we see today.

The earth standing out of the water and in the water is a description of the deep filling the universe found in *Genesis 1:2*. Noah's whole world did not perish; a remnant survived. In fact the days of Noah- literally continued. Noah lived 350 years this side of the flood. An often overlooked fact is the *days of Noah* include Genesis chapter 6 and Genesis 11. Noah *was a citizen of Babel, and he died just 2 years before Abraham was born.*

Genesis 7:6 And Noah was six hundred years old when the flood of waters was upon the earth.

Genesis 9:28-29 And Noah lived after the flood three hundred and fifty years. 29 And all the days of Noah were nine hundred and fifty years: and he died.

Opposing Views

§

SALIENT VERSES FOR THE YOUNG earth theory are presented below. Their point being: the scripture puts marriage, (men and women) in the beginning. Since God created Adam and Eve 6,000 years ago- And this beginning is emphatically believed to be *Ge.1:1*; therefore, evidence for the 6,000 year old earth with no recreation is found here.

Matthew 19:4 *And he answered and said unto them, Have ye not read, that he which made them **at the beginning** made them male and female,*

Mark 10:6 *But from the beginning of the creation God made them male and female.*

Numerous scriptures use the word **beginning** where the context is obviously explained right in the verse. There are passages, however, where the context is understood from previously established knowledge. Rightly dividing the word of truth includes understanding the context. God always uses *beginning*- as the origin of something, but *beginning* -does not always refer back to *Genesis 1:1*. Consider the exact same expression **at the beginning** used in *1 Chron. 17:9-10*.

1 Chronicles 17:9-10 *Also I will ordain a place for my people Israel, and will plant them, and they shall dwell in their place, and shall be moved* *no more; neither shall the children of wickedness waste them any more, as **at the beginning**, 10 And since the time that I commanded judges to be over my people Israel. Moreover I will subdue all thine enemies. Furthermore I tell thee that the LORD will build thee an house.*

Was Israel wasted in the creation week? Of course not; God speaks about creating the state of Israel. Interpretation based on information the reader already knows about Israel; therefore, we conclude this **at the beginning** is in the dispensation of the patriarchs.

In much the same way, believers in the Gap concluded *Mt.19:4* defines the beginning as an age immediately after the voiding of the earth. In contrast the creationists insist this is proof text for the 6,000 year old earth, because they believe God created the earth the same week as he made Adam and Eve.

Within this debate, it's important to remember no one doubts God created Adam and Eve only 6,000 years ago- Nor does anyone doubt the contents of the 2nd heavens are only 6,000 years old. Only the earth is older. In my opinion, it is remarkable creationists view *Mt.19:4 and Mk.10: 6* as absolute evidence for a young earth. After careful consideration, one should, at least, acknowledge the alternative explanation as a possibility. God voiding his original earth is based on a thoughtful examination of a large body of scriptural evidence.

THOUGHT TO PONDER:

Thought to ponder: If one commits to interpreting the beginning as a point in time only 6,000 years ago, does this mean *John 1;1-2* -is referencing 4,000 BC ?

John 1:1-2 In the beginning was the Word, and the Word was with God, and the Word was God. 2 The same was in the beginning with God.

ANOTHER OPPOSING SCRIPTURAL PROOF TEXT:

Exodus 20:11 For in six days the LORD made heaven and earth, the sea, and all that in them is, and rested the seventh day: wherefore the LORD blessed the sabbath day, and hallowed it.

Gap fact believers can answer this as follows: God did indeed make this current universe (heaven) in six days. **A distinction should be observed in the word *make*- opposed to *create*.** One can make something out of material that already exists. Creation is from nothing. In fact, the word create is not used until days five and six- when God makes animal and human life. If the words create and made are always synonymous, why does God use both words in the same sentence?

*Genesis 2:3 And God blessed the seventh day, and sanctified it: because that in it he had rested from all his work which God **created and made.***

Consider also that God did not make or create anything on the third day. Genesis 1:9-13 is the account of God's actions on the third day.

*Genesis 9-13 And God said, Let the waters under the heaven be gathered together unto one place, and let the dry land appear: and it was so. **10** And God called the dry land Earth; and the gathering together of the waters called he Seas: and God saw that it was good. **11** And God said, Let the earth bring forth grass, the herb yielding seed, and the fruit tree yielding fruit after his kind, whose seed is in itself, upon the earth: and it was so. **12** And the earth brought forth grass, and herb yielding seed after his kind, and the tree yielding fruit, whose seed was in itself, after his kind: and God saw that it was good. **13 And the evening and the morning were the third day.***

* 1st day: Let there be light.
* 2nd day: God made the firmament.
* 3rd day: Nothing made or created.

- 4th day: God made moon, sun, stars.
- 5th day: God creates aquatic life and birds.
- 6th day: God made land animals; creates man.
- 7th day: God rests.

ANOTHER "PROOF TEXT" COMMONLY CITED:

Revelation 21:1 *And I saw a new heaven and a new earth: for the first heaven and the first earth were passed away; and there was no more sea.*

The voiding of the earth in *Genesis 1:2* did not dissolve the planet nor did the physical elements disappear; thus, the first earth or planet still exists. God submerged earth in water and everything on the surface was obliterated. This is still the first earth.

Revelation 21:1 is not an argument against the gap. As this study has stated numerous times, the earth was created in verse 1 which is not part of the creation week. The earth was made void in verse 2. On day 3 God gathered the waters covering the earth into one place making the dry land appear, thus the earth was already in existence-although it had been submerged in water.

THOUGHT TO PONDER.

God created darkness, but scripture does not record when he did it. Clearly darkness existed before God made light.

Isaiah 45:7 *I form the light, and create darkness: I make peace, and create evil: I the LORD do all these things.*

Genesis Chapter 1

SCRIPTURAL RECORD OF CREATION:
*GENESIS 1:1-28 IN THE BEGINNING **God created** the heaven and the earth.*

GAP

2 And the earth was without form, and void; and darkness was upon the face of the deep. And the Spirit of God moved upon the face of the waters.

DAY 1 (LIGHT)

*3 And God said, **Let there be light:** and there was light. 4 And God saw the light, that it was good: and God divided the light from the darkness. 5 And God called the light Day, and the darkness he called Night. And the evening and the morning were **the first day.***

DAY 2 (GOD MAKES THE FIRMAMENT)

*6 And God said, Let there be a firmament in the midst of the waters, and let it divide the waters from the waters. 7 And **God made the***

firmament, *and divided the waters which were under the firmament from the waters which were above the firmament: and it was so. 8 And God called the firmament Heaven. And the evening and the morning* **were the second day.**

Day 3 (Nothing made or created)

Genesis 1:9-13 *And God said, Let the waters under the heaven be gathered together unto one place, and let the dry land appear: and it was so. 10 And God called the dry land Earth; and the gathering together of the waters called he Seas: and God saw that it was good. 11 And God said, Let the earth bring forth grass, the herb yielding seed, and the fruit tree yielding fruit after his kind, whose seed is in itself, upon the earth: and it was so. 12 And the earth brought forth grass, and herb yielding seed after his kind, and the tree yielding fruit, whose seed was in itself, after his kind: and God saw that it was good. 13 And the evening and the morning were the third day.*

Day 4 (God makes the Sun, Moon, Stars)

14 And God said, Let there be lights in the firmament of the heaven to divide the day from the night; and let them be for signs, and for seasons, and for days, and years: 15 And let them be for lights in the firmament of the heaven to give light upon the earth: and it was so. **16 And God made two great lights; the greater light to rule the day, and the lesser light to rule the night: he made the stars also.** *17 And God set them in the firmament of the heaven to give light upon the earth, 18 And to rule over the day and over the night, and to divide the light from the darkness: and God saw that it was good. 19 And the evening and the morning were* **the fourth day.**

DAY 5 (GOD CREATES AQUATIC LIFE, BIRDS

*20 And God said, Let the waters bring forth abundantly the moving creature that hath life, and fowl that may fly above the earth in the open firmament of heaven. 21 And **God created great whales, and every living creature that moveth, which the waters brought forth abundantly, after their kind, and every winged fowl after his kind:** and God saw that it was good. 22 And God blessed them, saying, Be fruitful, and multiply, and fill the waters in the seas, and let fowl multiply in the earth. 23 And the evening and the morning were **the fifth day.***

DAY 6 GOD MAKES ANIMALS. GOD CREATES MAN.

*24 And God said, Let the earth bring forth the living creature after his kind, cattle, and creeping thing, and beast of the earth after his kind: and it was so. 25 And God **made the beast of the earth** after his kind, and cattle after their kind, and every thing that creepeth upon the earth after his kind: and God saw that it was good. 26 And God said, Let us make man in our image, after our likeness: and let them have dominion over the fish of the sea, and over the fowl of the air, and over the cattle, and over all the earth, and over every creeping thing that creepeth upon the earth. 27 So **God created man in his own image, in the image** of God created he him; male and female created he them. 28 And God blessed them, and God said unto them, Be fruitful, and multiply, and replenish the earth, and subdue it: and have dominion over the fish of the sea, and over the fowl of the air, and over every living thing that moveth upon the earth.*

    ***Genesis 1:29-31** And God said, Behold, I have given you every herb bearing seed, which is upon the face of all the earth, and every tree, in the which is the fruit of a tree yielding seed; to you it shall be for meat. 30 And to every beast of the earth, and to every fowl of the air, and to every thing* *that creepeth upon the earth, wherein there is life, I have given every green herb for meat: and it was so.* **31** *And God saw every thing that he had made, and, behold, it was very good. And the evening and the morning were* **the sixth day.**

Light Years

§

BOTH YOUNG EARTH THEORISTS AND gap fact believers need an answer when it comes to stellar distance and time. How can the visible universe be only 6,000 years old, when science convincingly asserts that light from stars and galaxies takes millions of years to arrive on earth?

Light travels at 186,000 miles per second. Astronomers compute the distance to a star according to light years, in other words, how long it takes light emanating from a particular star to arrive on earth. The nearest star (after our sun) is Alpha Centauri which is 4.4 light years away. Star light from the center of our own Milky Way Galaxy is 27,000 years away. Time and distances become literally astronomical from there on. Galaxies exist whose light is millions of years old. Light from the Sombrero galaxy (M104) takes over 60million years to arrive on earth, yet we see it today. The problem is obvious, how can the universe be only 6,000 years old.

True science agrees with the Bible. And Christians need not view science as an enemy. And although evolution is complete foolishness, light years and star distances could well be accurate. Nothing about light years contradicts a 6,000 year old universe. How can this be?

Genesis 1:14-19 *And God said, Let there be lights in the firmament of the heaven to divide the day from the night; and let them be for signs,* *and for seasons, and for days, and years:* **15 And let them be for lights in the firmament of the heaven to give light upon the earth: and it was so.** *16 And God made two great lights; the greater light to rule the day, and the lesser light to rule the night:* **he made the stars also. 17 And God set them in the firmament of the heaven to give light upon the earth, 18 And to rule over the day and over the night, and to divide the light from the darkness**: *and God saw that it was good. 19 And the evening and the morning were the fourth day.*

On the 4ᵗʰ day of the creation week, God made the contents of the universe. He made the moon, sun, and stars. This includes many billions of galaxies. Everything in the universe (except earth) was made on the 4ᵗʰ day.

Look closely at *Genesis 1:14-19*. Everything that gives light was created to minister to the earth. The very purpose of the stars, no matter how far away, was to give light upon the earth. God made the stars' light already visible to earth the moment he made the stars. All the action (light that earth can see) in the universe, from quasars to supernovas, from comets, meteors, to unexplainable phenomena- God made to minister to the earth in various capacities- and to divide light from darkness.

Thought to ponder: It is interesting to examine the construction of the word universe. **Uni** and **verse,** uni- meaning one- and verse meaning text. God made everything in one verse, hence we have the uni-verse; therefore, when scientists refer to the cosmos as the universe, they are unconsciously referring to *Genesis 1:1*.

Genesis 1:1 *In the beginning God created the heaven and the earth.*

Replenish

*GENESIS **1:28** AND GOD BLESSED them, and God said unto them, Be fruitful, and multiply, and replenish the earth, and subdue it: and have dominion over the fish of the sea, and over the fowl of the air, and over every living thing that moveth upon the earth.*

The first definition of the word replenish- is to put back or fill again. It is argued that ***replenish*** can also mean to fill (which is true). Thus *Ge.1:28* is not evidence for a pre-adamite earth. *Genesis 1:28-* by itself- is not proof text. And no one who believes in the Gap ever believed the doctrine based on this verse alone.

Bible students know the wisest way to interpret scripture is to let the Bible interpret itself. **God uses the word replenish only seven times.** The verses where replenish is used (after Genesis 1:28) clearly mean to refill or put back. Compares this to the word **fill used 249 times**. If all replenish means is to fill- why did God use the word replenish? Obviously, God has serious, discriminating reasons to use the word replenish instead of using the word *fill*.

Below are the 7 verses where God uses the word ***replenish***. For the 249 times God uses the word ***fill***, the reader is encouraged to examine them on his/her own.

Genesis 1:28 *And God blessed them, and God said unto them, Be fruitful, and multiply, and replenish the earth, and subdue it: and have* *dominion over the fish of the sea, and over the fowl of the air, and over every living thing that moveth upon the earth.*

Genesis 9:1 *And God blessed Noah and his sons, and said unto them, Be fruitful, and multiply, and replenish the earth.*

Isaiah 2:6 *Therefore thou hast forsaken thy people the house of Jacob, because they be replenished from the east, and are soothsayers like the Philistines, and they please themselves in the children of strangers.*

Isaiah 23:2 *Be still, ye inhabitants of the isle; thou whom the merchants of Zidon, that pass over the sea, have replenished.*

Jeremiah 31:25 *For I have satiated the weary soul, and I have replenished every sorrowful soul.*

Ezekiel 26:2 *Son of man, because that Tyrus hath said against Jerusalem, Aha, she is broken that was the gates of the people: she is turned unto me: I shall be replenished, now she is laid waste:*

Ezekiel 27:25 *The ships of Tarshish did sing of thee in thy market: and thou wast replenished, and made very glorious in the midst of the seas.*

Even ardent defenders of the KJV go to great academic lengths to show ***replenish*** does not always mean refill. They will appeal to the etymological history of the word ***replenish***, in an attempt to prove replenish only meant *to fill* in the 17th century. This however is not true. Replenish appeared **in a poem in 1612**. It appears again in Pepys' Diary, where he says: '*buy to replenish the stores*'.

The Oxford English Dictionary comes out every 10 years like a census; it is an authority on the English language. The OED provides an etymological historical reference from 1612 and 1632 where replenish was used in a refilling context. So what does this do to the claim that it was never used this way? And even if it wasn't (but it was) why would it surprise anyone the KJV was ahead of worldly, secular writers? Because after all is said and done concerning the word replenish, it is the King James Bible, as usual, that gives scholars an etymological pain in their frontal lobes.

Romans 11:33 *O the depth of the riches both of the wisdom and knowledge of God! how unsearchable are his judgments, and his ways past finding out!*

Angels

No matter what one's position is on the Gap- some speculation is required concerning the angels. God does not record chapter and verse for creating angels, as he does for man. But clearly angelic life exists. A passage from the book of Job adds insight. Notice angels already existed when God created this earth; they shout for joy when they saw it. Scripture identifies them as the morning stars.

Job 38:4-7 Where wast thou when I laid the foundations of the earth? declare, if thou hast understanding. 5 Who hath laid the measures thereof, if thou knowest? or who hath stretched the line upon it? 6 Whereupon are the foundations thereof fastened? or who laid the corner stone thereof; 7 When the morning stars sang together, and all the sons of God shouted for joy?

Some angels are imprisoned in hell right now, while other evil angels are free to wage war against mankind. We are not told exactly when the angels sinned and went to war with God, but scriptures make clear they did, and they continue in rebellion till at least the Tribulation. It appears this war has raged much longer than 6,000 years.

Revelation 12:7-9 And there was war in heaven: Michael and his angels fought against the dragon; and the dragon fought and his angels, 8 And prevailed not; neither was their place found any more in heaven. 9

And the great dragon was cast out, that old serpent, called the Devil, and Satan, which deceiveth the whole world: he was cast out into the earth, and his angels were cast out with him.

Matthew 25:41 *Then shall he say also unto them on the left hand, Depart from me, ye cursed, into everlasting fire, prepared for the devil and his angels:*

1 Corinthians 6:3 *Know ye not that we shall judge angels? how much more things that pertain to this life?*

From *Revelation 12:3-4*, we speculate one third of all the angels joined with Lucifer. If that inference is correct, it is very alarming. God often likens angels to stars, if the number of physical stars in the universe compares to the number of living angels, then their number is astronomically huge! Consider our Milky Way Galaxy consists of approximately four hundred billion stars. Consider also there are billions of other galaxies in the 2nd heaven.

Revelation 12:3-4 *And there appeared another wonder in heaven; and behold a great red dragon, having seven heads and ten horns, and seven crowns upon his heads. 4 And his tail drew the third part of the stars of heaven, and did cast them to the earth: and the dragon stood before the woman which was ready to be delivered, for to devour her child as soon as it was born.*

THOUGHT TO PONDER: OUT OF TIME

Without digressing into a tedious, philosophical time study- God created Adam about 4000 BC. Something happening *out of time* is an event which happens outside the boundaries of datable events. Bible students only have a little slice of eternity, 7,000 years, where we can locate events in time. Thus either end of eternity's time line, could be considered *out of time*.

Job 22 contains a curious passage on a civilization destroyed by a flood. Admittedly, Job's generation is not very distant from Noah's flood; so it is reasonable to presume the passage deals with Noah's antediluvian generation. Never the less- the passage below may be commenting on preadamite era.

Job 22:15-20 Hast thou marked the old way which wicked men have trodden? 16 **Which were cut down out of time, whose foundation was overflown with a flood:** *17 Which said unto God, Depart from us: and what can the Almighty do for them? 18 Yet he filled their houses with good things: but the counsel of the wicked is far from me. 19 The righteous see it, and are glad: and the innocent laugh them to scorn. 20 Whereas our substance is not cut down, but the remnant of them the fire consumeth.*

In context one of Job's friends, Eliphaz, engages in dialog with Job. Eliphaz comments on wicked men who lived in the past, men who suffered the judgment of a flood. The question is which flood, Noah's flood or the Gap's universal flood?

Verse 16 is the provocative verse. These men were *cut down out of time*. What does this mean? The Gap literally took place out of time, if we define time as the measure of biblical world history.

The idea becomes even more intriguing when we look at the words *cut down*. These are the same words used to define Lucifer's fall; a fall that took place out of time.

Isaiah 14:12   How art thou fallen from heaven, O Lucifer, son of the morning! how art thou **cut down** to the ground, which didst weaken the nations!

Lucifer's Fall

§

FOR INFORMATION ABOUT SATAN'S ORIGINAL position with God, and the age in which he lived, we turn to the prophets. Isaiah and Ezekiel tell us Lucifer once held high favor with God, his status and position was lofty and extraordinary. But Lucifer was not satisfied; he wanted more.

In an age long ago, God called Satan Lucifer. His name means *light bearer or the shining one.* Lucifer's rebellion centered on his own pride. It seems Lucifer wanted equality with Jesus Christ; he wanted to be worshipped. At the time of Lucifer's fall, that meant he wanted the adoration and worship from angels. *Isaiah 14:12-15* addresses Lucifer's great rebellion. Apparently Lucifer persuaded a significant number of angels to join in his opposition toward God.

Chronologically, in the Bible, Satan first appears in Genesis 3; he is called the serpent. Obviously, Satan's fall already happened because he is tempting Eve to sin against God. Thus we conclude Lucifer's fall preceded the fall of mankind.

*Isaiah 14:12-15 How art thou fallen from heaven, O Lucifer, son of the morning! how art thou cut down to the ground, **which didst weaken the nations! 13** For thou hast said in thine heart, **I will ascend into heaven,** I will exalt my throne above the stars of God: I will sit also upon the mount of the congregation, **in the sides of the north: 14** I will ascend* *above the heights of the clouds; I will be like the most High.* **15** *Yet thou shalt be brought down to hell, to the sides of the pit.*

Notice Lucifer boasts he will *ascend into heaven.* God's throne and temple exist in the 3rd heaven, in the sides of the north. The singular heaven is an important reference. In the beginning there was one heaven (not heavens). Scripture is consistent when identifying the era Lucifer fell. *Genesis 1:1* is probably the most misquoted verse in the Bible. How long did it take Lucifer to corrupt the meaning of texts in new bible versions? Answer: One verse.

Genesis 1:1 *In the beginning God created the heaven and the earth.*

Lucifer's war with God resulted in cataclysmic consequences, literally a destroyed universe and the fall of a considerable number of angels. This war ended when God flooded out the heaven and voided the earth. Then God started over by recreating the earth and creating man in his own image. After Lucifer's fall, three heavens exist. Today the sides of the north are in the 3rd heaven.

Implicit in *Isaiah 14:12-15* is the fact Lucifer weakened the nations. These nations are collateral damage with Lucifer's fall. What nations? The nations weakened due to Lucifer's rebellion. These nations existed during Lucifer's rebellion.

An inhabited earth in eternity past- an earth where Lucifer held a very high position, gives insight into Satan's claim the world is his *Matthew. 4:8-9.* It also explains the intense jealousy he holds toward mankind. What was once the home of angels, God gave to an entirely new creation, a being created in the God's image, a being capable of reproducing images of God! As great as angels are, they are not created in the image of God. Nor do they reproduce.

Matthew 4:8-9 *Again, the devil taketh him up into an exceeding high mountain, and sheweth him all the kingdoms of the world, and the glory of them;* **9** *And saith unto him, All these things will I give thee, if thou wilt fall down and worship me.*

Although Satan failed to acquire his own throne in the sides of the north, he remains active pursuing worship from human beings as well as angels. The passage below is loaded, cited to prove only the percentage of angels in league with Satan. Since angels are likened to stars, their total number could well be astronomical. *Revelation 12:3-4* declares the dragon drew 1/3 of the stars. The stars, here, are angels as they are in *Isaiah 14:13. Job 38:7, and Psalm 147:4.*

Revelation 12:3-4 *And there appeared another wonder in heaven; and behold a great red dragon, having seven heads and ten horns, and seven crowns upon his heads.* **4 And his tail drew the third part of the stars of heaven, and did cast them to the earth:** *and the dragon stood before the woman which was ready to be delivered, for to devour her child as soon as it was born.*

Job 38:7 *When the morning stars sang together, and all the sons of God shouted for joy?*

Psalms 147:4 *He telleth the number of the stars; he calleth them all by their names.*

King of Tyrus

Anointed Cherub

§

TYRUS MEANS 'TO DISTRESS'

SATAN'S WAS NOT ALWAYS A seven headed, legless serpent. Originally he was one of God's most beautiful creatures. The Lord actually calls him perfect in beauty and in all his ways, including wisdom. Lucifer may be the most powerful, smartest creature God ever created. In Ezekiel's description Lucifer is named king of Tyrus. Satan's title (before his fall) was *the anointed cherub that covereth*. It seems his duties included being in charge of God's throne room. At the time of Lucifer's fall, heaven's Mount Zion including God's Temple and throne were on earth. After Lucifer's fall God relocated this whole region to the 3rd heaven.

Although *Ezekiel 28:12-19* has an historical application to the human King of Tyrus, it's obvious the doctrinal application concerns Satan, because he was in the Garden of Eden. The only persons recorded to be in Eden were Adam, Eve and the Serpent. Additionally, God identifies the King of Tyrus as the anointed cherub. *Ezekiel 28:14*. The passage gives important insight into Lucifer's history.

Notice the anointed cherub walked in the midst of the stones of holy fire. Fire appears a natural part of Lucifer's habitat even before his fall. Leviathan breathing sparks of fire may be reminiscent of his past glory. Observe also the first ten verses in *Ezekiel 28* concern the **prince of Tyrus**, while the *28:12-15* concern the **king of Tyrus**. A prince, of course, is the son of a king; thus the passage discusses the Antichrist (serpent's seed) whose father is the anointed cherub. *Compare Ezekiel 28:1-10 to 2 Thessalonians 2:3-4.*

Ezekiel 28:12-19 *Son of man, take up a lamentation upon the king of Tyrus, and say unto him, Thus saith the Lord GOD; Thou sealest up the sum, full of wisdom, and perfect in beauty. **13** Thou hast been in Eden the garden of God; every precious stone was thy covering, the sardius, topaz, and the diamond, the beryl, the onyx, and the jasper, the sapphire, the emerald, and the carbuncle, and gold: the workmanship of thy tabrets and of thy pipes was prepared in thee in the day that thou wast created. **14** Thou art the anointed cherub that covereth; and I have set thee so: thou wast upon the holy mountain of God; thou hast walked up and down in the midst of the stones of fire. **15** Thou wast perfect in thy ways from the day that thou wast created, till iniquity was found in thee. **16 By the multitude of thy merchandise they have filled the midst of thee with violence, and thou hast sinned:** therefore I will cast thee as profane out of the mountain of God: and I will destroy thee, O covering cherub, from the midst of the stones of fire. **17** Thine heart was lifted up because of thy beauty, thou hast corrupted thy wisdom by reason of thy brightness: I will cast thee to the ground, I will lay thee before kings, that they may behold thee. **18 Thou hast defiled thy sanctuaries by the multitude of thine iniquities, by the iniquity of thy traffick;** therefore will I bring forth a fire from the midst of thee, it shall devour thee, and I will bring thee to ashes upon the earth in the sight of all them that behold thee. **19** All they that know thee among the people shall be astonished at thee: thou shalt be a terror, and never shalt thou be any more.*

Notice Satan defiled his own sanctuaries. And the multitude of his merchandise inspired sin and violence. These sanctuaries contributed to the original earth's society and culture. The sanctuaries somehow connected business and an economic system. Satan corrupted them through a multitude of iniquities. Curiously, God also says by the *iniquity of his traffick*. God uses the word traffick only five times in the Bible. Each use is connected with trading, merchandise, and economic dealings. In modern times the word traffic still defines the same activities

Satan desires worship. And in order to promote himself, he required wealth and power. This sounds amazingly reminiscent of human sin. Other scriptures also connect these original satanic sins with mankind. Have you ever wondered how the *love of money is the root of all evil*? The original money lover is the anointed cherub himself. And since Satan provoked Eve and Adam to sin- this sin is the root of all man's sinfulness.

1 Timothy 6:10 For the love of money is the root of all evil: which while some coveted after, they have erred from the faith, and pierced themselves through with many sorrows.

Prince of Tyrus

§

MONEY TRAFFICKING AND COMMERCE CONNECTS to the prince of Tyrus. And this prince is no mere mortal. After all his father, king of Tyrus, is the anointed cherub. The Cherub's son carries out ambitions of his father. Thus the prince of Tyrus is the Antichrist and seeks to rule the world. Compare *Ezekiel 29:2-9 with 2 Thessalonians 2:3-4.*

Contemplate business practices of the coming Antichrist. The Antichrist's primary action promoting the world's acceptance, even worship- is when he restructures the world's economic system. And the only prerequisite condition - global economic collapse. **Make no doubt about it- the coming Antichrist is an economic genius**. To *buy or sell* is a perfectly succinct definition of an economic system. And ultimately, it's an economy controlled by antichrist, just like an economy his father controlled in a previous age.

Revelation 13:16-18 And he causeth all, both small and great, rich and poor, free and bond, to receive a mark in their right hand, or in their foreheads: 18 And that no man might buy or sell, save he that had the mark, or the name of the beast, or the number of his name. 18 Here is wisdom. Let him that hath understanding count the number of the beast: for it is the number of a man; and his number is Six hundred threescore and six.

Ezekiel 28:2-9 *Son of man, say unto the **prince of Tyrus**, Thus saith the Lord GOD; Because thine heart is lifted up, and thou hast said, I am a God, I sit in the seat of God, in the midst of the seas; yet thou art a man, and not God, though thou set thine heart as the heart of God: **3** Behold, thou art wiser than Daniel; there is no secret that they can hide from thee: **4** With thy wisdom and with thine understanding thou hast gotten thee riches, and hast gotten gold and silver into thy treasures: **5** By thy great wisdom and by thy traffick hast thou increased thy riches, and thine heart is lifted up because of thy riches: **6** Therefore thus saith the Lord GOD; Because thou hast set thine heart as the heart of God; **7** Behold, therefore I will bring strangers upon thee, the terrible of the nations: and they shall draw their swords against the beauty of thy wisdom, and they shall defile thy brightness. **8** They shall bring thee down to the pit, and thou shalt die the deaths of them that are slain in the midst of the seas. **9** Wilt thou yet say before him that slayeth thee, **I am God? but thou shalt be a man,** and no God, in the hand of him that slayeth thee.*

2 Thessalonians 2:3-4 *Let no man deceive you by any means: for that day shall not come, except there come a falling away first, and that man of sin be revealed, the son of perdition; **4** Who opposeth and exalteth himself above all that is called God, or that is worshipped; so that he as God sitteth in the temple of God, shewing himself that he is God.*

A Previous Age

JEREMIAH 4:23-26 SISTER TEXT TO *Genesis 1:2, Ezekiel 28:12-19*, reveals much about God's original earth and world. The passage poses a conundrum for those who don't believe in the gap fact. Admittedly, I include some inference, but the alternatives of ignoring what Jeremiah writes- or reducing it to spiritualized fluff is worse.

Considering Jeremiah chapter 4 in context: God gives Judah a warning; imminent judgment is coming. Without repentance, Nebuchadnezzar invades and implements God's wrath and punishment. The Lord's chosen people endure their nation's destruction. Survivors become prisoners and removed into captivity. This is the gist of Jeremiah chapter 4. But in the middle of the ominous prophecy, Jeremiah says,

"I beheld the earth, and lo, it was without form, and void..." Unmistakably, this statement is a direct reference to Genesis 1:2

Genesis 1:2 *And the earth was without form, and void; and darkness was upon the face of the deep. And the Spirit of God moved upon the face of the waters.*

Jeremiah 4:23-26 *I beheld the earth, and, lo, it was without form, and void; and the heavens, and they had no light. 24 I beheld the mountains, and, lo, they trembled, and all the hills moved lightly. 25 I beheld, and, lo, there was no man, and all the birds of the heavens were fled. 26 I*

beheld, and, lo, the fruitful place was a wilderness, and all the cities thereof were broken down at the presence of the LORD, and by his fierce anger.

Why would God incorporate this statement into the prophetic warning? Obviously, Jeremiah was not alive in *Genesis 1:2.* The prophet experiences a vision much like Apostle John in the book of Revelation. The difference is John saw the future and Jeremiah saw the past.

Here is the conundrum for creationists (those not believing in the gap fact). Why does God even have Jeremiah say this? If one runs the passage to *Genesis.1:2,* (which all Bible students know they have to do.) what is God's point? How is the earth being without form and void relevant to Jeremiah 4? The whole chapter concerns judgment, especially punishment for rebellion and sin.

The point God makes to Judah is as follows: God reached a breaking point with a world in eternity past, and he flooded out his entire universe, and voided the original earth; don't think for a second God won't judge one nation. Just like Lucifer's and the angels' sinful behavior met with divine catastrophic judgment; so too will Judah's and Israel's.

The four *I beheld* statements in verses *4:23-26,* serve direct commentary on God's original world. The world he made void. A world holding cities, a fruitful place, mountains, and at least some animal life. Notice there was no man and no light. The birds being fled, implies that birds were once there. Let the Bible student consider:

* When was there no man?
* When was there no light?
* When were all the cities broken down?

And how do these statements relate to the earth being without form and void? God gives Jeremiah a vision when he voided the earth *Ge. 1:2*. The heavens had no light in *Genesis 1:2* only darkness on the face of the deep, and light was not created until *Ge. 1:3*. God created darkness before light, *Isaiah 45:7*.

God destroyed a civilization inhabited by angels. People don't think much about how and where angels live. But angels aren't sitting around on clouds playing harps. Some kind of societal habitation provided home to angels on the original earth, just as it now does in the 3rd heaven.

Curiosity about the Bible is spiritually healthy. In order to have an engaged, maturing relationship with the Bible, one must think about what God wrote. Knowledge often generates questions, and questions inspire thinking. Since Lucifer once lived in a holy relationship with God; to inquire about his past seems important. It's amazing how uncurious Christians are about the Bible. Why the fall of Lucifer is so seldom considered is but one example.

Thought to Ponder

Solomon teaches everything that happened in the past, happens again in the future. This includes Lucifer trying to be like God. More specifically, the Antichrist tries to take the throne of Jesus Christ and rule the world from a temple.

Ecclesiastes 1:9-10 The thing that hath been, it is that which shall be; and that which is done is that which shall be done: and there is no new thing under the sun. 10 Is there any thing whereof it may be said, See, this is new? it hath been already of old time, which was before us.

Ecclesiastes 3:15 That which hath been is now; and that which is to be hath already been; and God requireth that which is past.

Music

§

SOMEONE ONCE SAID GOD APPOINTED Lucifer the first choir director or the master of music. That theory supposes a very good educated guess. According to *Ezekiel 28:13*, God's purpose for the anointed cherub included musical ability. Tabrets and pipes are musical devices. Music remains a powerful force provoking spiritual, emotional, and religious motivation. Music's divine purpose is to worship God, inspiring awe and adoration of Jesus Christ. It also promotes holy and righteous living in believers.

The opposite is also true. As mankind descends into an ever darker moral abyss, the world's entertainment becomes increasingly dedicated to celebrating sin. The days of benign or harmless musical enjoyments are rapidly ending. The whole of Man's musical creativity is turning to religious idolatry. As the world approaches Jesus Christ's 2nd Coming, music is devolving. Music either promotes God or stands against him. Modern love songs seem more like people worshipping each other than expressions of human affection. Disturbingly, more and more "Christian" songs sound increasingly like the world. Listen closely to the lyrics- are they written to a human lover or to God? And beware it takes more than correct words to make godly music. Rhythm, beat, and arrangement matter. Music even without human voice creates mood altering and emotional change. Symphonic, even classical orchestra inspires good as well as evil. That's why music is so important for movies and media productions. The power music incites should be handled responsibly and righteously, otherwise it becomes a perversion of God's intended purpose. In the end, Christ rejecting human genius perverts and redirects music to praise and worship Satan.

PSALM *150* SOON TO BE REPLACED BY DANIEL *3:4-6*

Ezekiel 28:13 the workmanship of thy tabrets and of thy pipes was prepared in thee in the day that thou wast created. 14 Thou art the anointed cherub that covereth.

Daniel 3:4-6 *Then an herald cried aloud, To you it is commanded, O people, nations, and languages, 5 That at what time ye hear the sound of the cornet, flute, harp, sackbut, psaltery, dulcimer, and all kinds of musick, ye fall down and worship the golden image that Nebuchadnezzar the king hath set up: 6 And whoso falleth not down and worshippeth shall the same hour be cast into the midst of a burning fiery furnace.*

Psalms 150:1-6 *Praise ye the LORD. Praise God in his sanctuary: praise him in the firmament of his power. 2 Praise him for his mighty acts: praise him according to his excellent greatness. 3 Praise him with the sound of the trumpet: praise him with the psaltery and harp. 4 Praise him with the timbrel and dance: praise him with stringed instruments and organs. 5 Praise him upon the loud cymbals: praise him upon the high sounding cymbals. 6 Let every thing that hath breath praise the LORD. Praise ye the LORD.*

THOUGHT TO PONDER

Satan is far more interested in Sunday morning than Saturday night. Satan's arena is spiritual and religious. Much of what the old serpent gets blamed for is actually inspired by man's own flesh: Drunkenness, sexual sin, drugs, gluttony, greed, etc. The lust of eye, and the pride of life *1 John. 2:16-* are directly motivated by mankind's own sinful desires. If Satan can't receive worship, his next objective persuades people to deny Jesus Christ. This followed closely by providing false doctrines to confuse and mislead people (including Christians). From full blown occult religion to Hollywood entertainment; hence the ever increasing fascination with death, demons, ghosts, vampires, and false perceptions of life after death. And false religions and cults that base their faith on not believing Jesus Christ is God. As the 2nd Coming of Jesus looms ever closer, the enemies of Christ become more overt and violent. Islamic doctrine and terrorism are but one example; with more to come- much more. The steadily increasing hatred of true Christianity, Jews, and the denial and/ or replacement of the perfectly preserved God's word, King James Bible -are thematic in the end times.

Cherub's Physical Appearance

THE BIBLE MENTIONS THREE CLASSES of angelic beings: Seraphim *Isaiah 6*, Cherubim, and Angels. *(Cherub is singular; cherubim is plural.)* Technically Satan is not an angel; he is a cherub. Some distinctions between the creatures appear as follows: Seraphim and cherubim have wings while angels do not have wings. Angels are associated or likened to stars. The Bible mentions only 5 cherubim, and only 2 Seraphim. All Cherubim are involved with God's throne room, sort of an inner circle of beings closest to God, consequently they appear to have great authority and more power than angels. In Ezekiel, Cherubim literally transport God's throne. *Ezekiel chapters 1, 10*

LIVING CHERUBIM

Scripture describes living cherubim in *Ezekiel 1 and 10*. Within these chapters scripture reveals cherubim transporting God's throne. When joined together, Cherubim exhibit an extraordinary metamorphosis; literally transforming into a unique being. The cherubim collectively become one living creature *(Ezekiel 10:15)*. Observe when the cherubim hold hands, each one has 4 faces: each individual cherub has the face of a man, lion, ox, and eagle. This totals 16 faces, a marvel of God's creation for sure.

We also learn separated cherubim (that is when they are not holding hands) have only one face. Comparing scripture with scripture reveals a single cherub has the face of an ox. Simply juxtapose *Ezekiel 1:10, with Ezekiel 10:14.* God uses the word **ox** in *1:10,* but substitutes the word *cherub in 10:14.* Thus we learn the independent visage and/or appearance of a single cherub is an ox.

Ezekiel 1:10 *As for the likeness of their faces, they four had the face of a man, and the face of a lion, on the right side: and they four had the face of an **ox** on the left side; they four also had the face of an eagle.*

Ezekiel 10:14 *And every one had four faces: the first face was the face of a **cherub,** and the second face was the face of a man, and the third the face of a lion, and the fourth the face of an eagle.*

Ezekiel 10:15 *And the cherubims were lifted up. This is the living creature that I saw by the river of Chebar.*

Recollecting God declared Lucifer perfect in beauty, one may ask, how an ox could be beautiful. Good question, but remember our only point of reference is the ox common to cattle. Those creatures may resemble a cherub no more than a gorilla does a man. Furthermore, consider the vast differences in human appearances. Although all humans have the same basic physical attributes: two eyes, two ears, a mouth, teeth, hair, etc. Some people are very beautiful and others may be grotesquely ugly, even deformed. Curiously, however, when God cursed the serpent, the first thing he says is- *cursed above all cattle.* As one continues thinking through the ox description, remember when Moses delayed in coming down from the mountain, after receiving the 10 Commandments? The people made a golden calf to worship.

More than 650 years later, after Israel divided into two nations, Israel and Judah. The wicked king Jeroboam set up two golden calves. One in the city of Bethel and the other in Dan. Then he fashioned a perverted false Judaism giving Israel an alternative (more fun) religion than the Bible based worship in Jerusalem. The northern kingdom embraced the idolatrous cows for the next several hundred years. And even in modern times, Hinduism regards the cow as sacred. As perplexing as it may be, the world has exhibited *holy cow* issues more than a few times over the last 3,000 years.

Genesis 3:14 And the LORD God said unto the serpent, Because thou hast done this, thou art cursed above all cattle, and above every beast of the field; upon thy belly shalt thou go, and dust shalt thou eat all the days of thy life:

Exodus 32:4 And he received them at their hand, and fashioned it with a graving tool, after he had made it a molten calf: and they said, These be thy gods, O Israel, which brought thee up out of the land of Egypt.

1 Kings 12:28-29 Whereupon the king took counsel, and made two calves of gold, and said unto them, It is too much for you to go up to Jerusalem: behold thy gods, O Israel, which brought thee up out of the land of Egypt. 29 And he set the one in Bethel, and the other put he in Dan.

CHERUBIM SCULPTURE

Numerous scriptures present sculptured or statues of Cherubim. King Solomon gives a cherub's best description when he constructed two sculpture replicas to adorn the temple. These cherubim statues were not worshiped! In fact, Solomon placed them inside the temple's inner sanctuary to be seen only by God. The only person to see them was the high priest one day a year when he visited the holy of holies on the Day of Atonement.

Scripture describes these two cherubim in precise mathematical terms. Ten cubits tall (15 feet) with wings 5 cubits wide (7.5 feet) one wing on each side. Since God designed the temple with such intricate detail, these replica cherubim are most likely the actual size of living cherubim. Most everything about the temple on earth is designed to mirror or shadow God's temple in the 3rd heaven located on the sides of the north. God's temple in heaven is made without hands, built by God. One significant difference between earth's and heaven's temple; however, heaven's temple contains God's Throne.

1 Kings 6:23-28 And within the oracle he made two cherubims of olive tree, each ten cubits high. 24 And five cubits was the one wing of the cherub, and five cubits the other wing of the cherub: from the uttermost part of the one wing unto the uttermost part of the other were ten cubits. 25 And the other cherub was ten cubits: both the cherubims were of one measure and one size. 26 The height of the one cherub was ten cubits, and so was it of the other cherub. 27 And he set the cherubims within the inner house: and they stretched forth the wings of the cherubims, so that the wing of the one touched the one wall, and the wing of the other cherub touched the other wall; and their wings touched one another in the midst of the house. 28 And he overlaid the cherubims with gold.

2 Chronicles 3:10-13 And in the most holy house he made two cherubims of image work, and overlaid them with gold. 11 And the wings of the cherubims were twenty cubits long: one wing of the one cherub was five cubits, reaching to the wall of the house: and the other wing was likewise five cubits, reaching to the wing of the other cherub. 12 And one wing of the other cherub was five cubits, reaching to the wall of the house: and the other wing was five cubits also, joining to the wing of the other cherub. 13 The wings of these cherubims spread themselves forth twenty cubits: and they stood on their feet, and their faces were inward.

Revelation 7:15 Therefore are they before the throne of God, and serve him day and night in his temple: and he that sitteth on the throne shall dwell among them.

Much smaller sculptures of cherubim rest on the mercy seat that sits atop the Ark of the Covenant. Like the larger images, these cherubim remained in the holy of holies and were never available to public viewing. Moses constructed the cherubim, the Ark of the Covenant, and the mercy seat during the days when God delivered the Jews from Egypt- for use in the tabernacle. The same Ark of the Covenant remained throughout the entire time Israel and Judah exercise temple worship, about 1,500 years: this included Moses' tabernacle, Solomon's temple, Zerubbabel's temple, and in New Testament times Herod's temple.

Exodus 25:17-21 And thou shalt make a mercy seat of pure gold: two cubits and a half shall be the length thereof, and a cubit and a half the breadth thereof. 18 And thou shalt make two cherubims of gold, of beaten work shalt thou make them, in the two ends of the mercy seat. 19 And make one cherub on the one end, and the other cherub on the other end: even of the mercy seat shall ye make the cherubims on the two ends thereof. 20 And the cherubims shall stretch forth their wings on high, covering the mercy seat with their wings, and their faces shall look one to another; toward the mercy seat shall the faces of the cherubims be. 21 And thou shalt put the mercy seat above upon the ark; and in the ark thou shalt put the testimony that I shall give thee.

THOUGHT TO PONDER

Cherubim appear first in the Bible immediately after Adam's and Eve's expulsion from the Garden of Eden. God positions Cherubim, armed with a flaming sword, to stop them from eating from the Tree of Life. Had any creature eaten from the tree, they would live forever- even in a spiritually lost, fallen condition. Considering the power of cherubim compared to human beings' weakness (especially only one man and one woman) doesn't it seems extraordinary God took such extreme measures to prevent anyone from eating from the Tree of Life? Rather like going deer hunting with a nuclear weapon.

Out of the 69 times Cherubim appear in the Bible, this is the only place the word is capitalized.

Genesis 3:22-24 And the LORD God said, Behold, the man is become as one of us, to know good and evil: and now, lest he put forth his hand, and take also of the tree of life, and eat, and live for ever: **23** Therefore the LORD God sent him forth from the garden of Eden, to till the ground from whence he was taken. **24** So he drove out the man; and he placed at the east of the garden of Eden **Cherubims, and a flaming sword which turned every way, to keep the way of the tree of life.**

The Serpent's Curse

LUCIFER'S PHYSICAL TRANSFORMATION

SATAN FIRST APPEARS IN GENESIS 3; there he is called the serpent. Obviously, Satan's fall already occurred because he is tempting Eve to sin against God. There is nothing good or holy about the serpent in Genesis 3.

Genesis 3:1 Now the serpent was more subtil than any beast of the field which the LORD God had made. And he said unto the woman, Yea, hath God said, Ye shall not eat of every tree of the garden?

Notice God does not say the serpent is a beast of the field; rather the serpent is segregated into a class by itself. This serpent is not a snake (reptile) any more than Jesus is a lamb (small farm animal) it is a reference to character and type. The serpent is the devil. When the Bible introduces the serpent in Genesis 3, he is already in rebellion against God and tempting mankind to join him; therefore, Lucifer's fall preceded God creating Adam and Eve.

Interpreting the passage as Eve conversing with a snake is hugely incorrect. Furthermore, the Bible tells exactly how the devil appears to human beings. He appears as an angel of light. Every time angels shows up in the Bible they are men without wings. Rarely do persons to whom they appear recognize them as angels. And Satan himself is called a man in *Isaiah14:16*; therefore, Eve is conversing with a man.

Equally important is the fact the serpent is smarter than Adam and Eve; overtly displaying evidence man does not have dominion over the serpent which proves (again) this serpent is not a beast of the field. (Dominion means to control, have authority over, to dominate)

*Genesis 1:28 And God blessed them, and God said unto them, Be fruitful, and multiply, and replenish the earth, and subdue it: **and have dominion over the fish of the sea, and over the fowl of the air, and over every living thing that moveth upon the earth.***

2 Corinthians 11:14 And no marvel; for Satan himself is transformed into an angel of light.

*Isaiah 14:16 They that see thee shall narrowly look upon thee, and consider thee, saying, **Is this the man** that made the earth to tremble, that did shake kingdoms;*

Hebrews 13:2 Be not forgetful to entertain strangers: for thereby some have entertained angels unawares.

THOUGHT TO PONDER

Do not presume all angels people entertain unawares are the good guys.

When Eve and Adam disobeyed God and ate from the tree of knowledge of good and evil- the Fall of mankind ensued. God's judgment inflicted consequences upon the serpent, men, women, and nature. Much could be said about the Fall; however, let us focus solely on God cursing the serpent. God curses Satan, not a snake! Again-endless theological and intellectual wrong turns commence if one concludes God curses some helpless animal. This error results in many unbelievers relegating the Fall of man to something akin to a Greek myth. Sadly, numerous Bible teachers fare little better.

Genesis 3:13-15 And the LORD God said unto the woman, What is this that thou hast done? And the woman said, The serpent beguiled me, and I did eat. **14 And the LORD God said unto the serpent, Because thou hast done this, thou art cursed above all cattle, and above every beast of the field; upon thy belly shalt thou go, and dust shalt thou eat all the days of thy life: 15 And I will put enmity between thee and the woman, and between thy seed and her seed; it shall bruise thy head, and thou shalt bruise his heel.**

Satan's glorious physical appearance changed forever. In other words he looked one way before the curse and another way after the curse. In my opinion, at this precise moment God transformed the most beautiful creature he ever created into a hideous legless dragon- Leviathan. And by the way, snakes don't eat dust; they are carnivores.

How this translates into Satan appearing to mankind today is unaltered. He appears as an angel of light or in the person of his son. Satan's physical manifestation is deceptive, always presenting an image of truth but always a lie. He is the master illusionist, smoke and mirrors and conspiracies are his forte. But his permanent actual state is described by God in *Job 41*.

Serpent's Seed

§

ANOTHER DARK TRUTH PRESENTS ITSELF when God curses the serpent. Observe the serpent produced a seed. There is no other way to interpret God saying *thy seed*; than to acknowledge the serpent has an offspring; therefore, since that time two evil beings exist, a serpent and the serpent's seed. Looking only at *Genesis 3:15*, the serpent's seed could come later, but the scripture speaks as if it already exists. Furthermore additional scriptures interpret the text. The unique mention of the *woman's seed* references the birth of Jesus Christ, a virgin birth via Mary.

Genesis 3:15 *And I will put enmity between thee and the woman, and between thy seed and her seed; it shall bruise thy head, and thou shalt bruise his heel.*

The Bible mentions no female species of any kind existing in a preadamite earth or previous age. Angels are male; the Bible mentions no female angel. Consequently, we read nowhere of any reproduction. It seems procreation began with Eve. When Satan heard God command Adam and Eve to be fruitful and multiply and replenish the earth, how did the serpent respond? What does the reader think? I believe he formulated an ambitious goal? If this female creature could procreate an image of God, perhaps she could produce an image of himself?

God has a Son; and Satan desires to be like God. God is a trinity; Satan does all he can to manifest himself as a trinity. The Antichrist is the literal, biological son of Satan, born of a woman. And just as the Bible equates God the Son (Jesus Christ) with God the Father. So does the Bible equate Satan the father with Satan the son, Antichrist. And the serpent is the father of it. This is the mystery of iniquity discussed in *2 Thessalonians 2:7-10*

John 8:44, 45 contains disturbing information. When Jesus rebukes the priests and Pharisees by telling them they are of their father the devil. He is saying their spiritual father is the devil. But his dialog continues and proclaims the devil was a *murderer from the beginning*. Then Jesus says a particular lie is the devil's own and the devil is the father of it. So the questions for Bible students are obvious.

1. Who was a murderer from the beginning?
2. And who or what is the devil's lie?

To help with interpretation remember Jesus Christ is literally called the truth *John 14:6*. In the darkest most opposite way Antichrist is called the lie. Satan's son is the lie. God's Son is the Truth.

John 8:44-45 *Ye are of your father the devil, and the lusts of your father ye will do.* **He was a murderer from the beginning,** *and abode not in the truth, because there is no truth in him.* **When he speaketh a lie, he speaketh of his own: for he is a liar, and the father of it.** *45 And because I tell you the truth, ye believe me not.*

1 John 3:12 *Not as Cain, who was of that wicked one, and slew his brother. And wherefore slew he him? Because his own works were evil, and his brother's righteous.*

2 Thessalonians 2:9-11 *Even him, whose coming is after the working of Satan with all power and signs and lying wonders, **10** And with all deceivableness of unrighteousness in them that perish; because they received* *not the love of the truth, that they might be saved.* **11** *And for this cause God shall send them strong delusion, that* **they should believe a lie:**

THE MURDERER FROM THE BEGINNING

Cain committed the first murder in human history, and he did it in beginning, thus *John 8:44* connects with *Genesis 4:8*.

Genesis 4:8 And Cain talked with Abel his brother: and it came to pass, when they were in the field, that Cain rose up against Abel his brother, and slew him.

Before Cain murdered his brother, God rejected Cain's offering but accepted Abel's offering. Thus the reason Cain was so angry. Cain's work offering typifies all false religions. The best men can do is not good enough, men need an offering God accepts. Good works mean nothing without first being accepted by God. Abel brought what God required, a blood offering. These two offerings basically represent the two ways human beings try to please God:

1. One group tries to earn heaven with good works.
2. The other group accepts God's offering and believes God's grace and mercy is the only way in.

Letting the Bible interpret itself, observe God's conversation with Cain-before the murder of Abel. God gives Cain advice and an opportunity for acceptance. But look closely at God's warning. If Cain continues in rebellion, what are the consequences?

NOUNS, PRONOUNS AND ANTECEDENTS.

Diagram sentence structure in *Genesis 4:6, 7*. Match each pronoun in the passage to the correct noun. There are 4 nouns: Lord, Cain, sin, door. There are 9 pronouns: One must go through the passage linking the pronouns to the correct noun (person, place, and thing). This may seem like an elementary school grammar lesson, but it forces one to a correct interpretation. Misidentifying the proper antecedent is a common error.

***Genesis 4:6-7** And the LORD said unto Cain, Why art thou wroth? and why is thy countenance fallen? 7 If thou doest well, shalt thou not be accepted? and if thou doest not well, sin lieth at the door. And unto thee shall be his desire, and thou shalt rule over him.*

Identifying the pronouns:

* thou= Cain
* thy= Cain
* thou= Cain
* thou= Cain
* thou= Cain
* thee= Cain
* his= sin
* thou= Cain
* him= sin

Interestingly, God chose the personal pronouns *his and him* to represent sin. God personified the word sin as if sin is a person. So continuing to examine the passage Bible students need to answer the following questions:

1. *Why art thou wroth?*
2. *Why is thy countenance fallen?*
3. *If thou doest well, shalt thou not be accepted?*

The obvious answers are Cain is angry because God did not accept his offering, but God accepted Abel's offering. Cain is jealous of Abel and mad at God. Cain worked hard to give God something, and he feels God is unjust for not accepting him. Cain's countenance is fallen for the same reasons. When God asks the third question, he gives Cain an opportunity to repent and do the right thing by bringing the offering God requires. If Cain did that, God would accept him.

Next God informs Cain about the consequences if he chooses to disobey. Bible students need to examine the consequences very closely. Since Cain did not do well, what does God say happened?

Consequences for Cain if he does not do well.

1. Sin lieth at the door.
2. Sin will have his desire with Cain.
3. Cain will rule over sin.

If a regular person succumbs to sin, no doubt sin will rule him/her. But in Cain's situation there is a far more nefarious consequence. Since Cain did not do well; Cain becomes the ruler of sin. The passage does not say that sin rules Cain. Disturbingly, it says the opposite. All this becomes the correlating texts for verses which identify the Antichrist, whom God calls the man of sin. Cain is the serpent's seed.

An immediate response to the hypothesis of Cain being the serpent's seed is, doesn't the Bible say Adam is Cain's father?

Genesis 4:1-2 *And Adam knew Eve his wife; and she conceived, and bare Cain, and said, I have gotten a man from the LORD. 2 And she again bare his brother Abel. And Abel was a keeper of sheep, but Cain was a tiller of the ground.*

The scripture does not plainly declare Adam is Cain's father; we infer that must be the case. But considering everything Jesus says about Cain, legitimate doubt is necessary. *Genesis 4:1-2* is perfectly true if Cain and Abel were fraternal twins with Adam's seed fathering Abel, and the serpent's seed fathering Cain.

Fraternal twins are "dizygotic," meaning they developed from two different eggs fertilized by two different sperm cells. It's very possible for two separate eggs to be fertilized by two different fathers. Fraternal twins are no more alike than individual brothers or sisters born at different times. While **identical** twins are "monozygotic" i.e., they develop from a single fertilized egg that split. Fraternal twins are more than twice as common as identical twins.

But wouldn't Eve know if the serpent was possibly the father? Not necessarily.

Sexual intercourse is not the only way for a female to become pregnant. Actually, conception can take place without a male being present; technically it is the male seed which needs be present. Laboratory insemination is just one example. The smartest creature God ever made is certainly creative enough to fertilize a woman's egg. When Eve says, *I have gotten a man from the LORD*, she is mistaken.

Man of Sin/Son of Perdition

§

Judas Iscariot is part two of this foreboding doctrine.

Cain Judas Iscariot

Best known for betraying Jesus, Judas Iscariot becomes the Bible's ultimate traitor. Judas Iscariot inhabits several dark and ominous prophecies in the Old Testament and becomes the epitome of evil in the New Testament. Consider Jesus' reference to his selection process for his Apostles. Jesus' declaration about Judas being a devil is far more than a figure of speech or a reference to a human being's moral or spiritual character.

John 6:70-71 Jesus answered them, Have not I chosen you twelve, and one of you is a devil? 71 He spake of Judas Iscariot the son of Simon: for he it was that should betray him, being one of the twelve.

Jesus provides more information on Judas just prior to his crucifixion. As Jesus prays for the Apostles, he identifies Judas as the *son of perdition*. Apostle Paul uses the same label to identify the Antichrist. The Bible uses the term, *son of perdition*, only twice. The definition of perdition is hell or damned. Scripture interprets itself and identifies Judas Iscariot as the Antichrist. Observe Judas is called the man of sin, which is very close to what God says about Cain becoming the ruler of sin. Jesus also said it would be better for Judas if he had never been born.

John 17:12 *While I was with them in the world, I kept them in thy name: those that thou gavest me I have kept, and none of them is lost,* **but the son of perdition;** *that the scripture might be fulfilled.*

2 Thessalonians 2:3-5 *Let no man deceive you by any means: for that day shall not come, except there come a falling away first, and* **that man of sin be revealed**, **the son of perdition;** *4 Who opposeth and exalteth himself above all that is called God, or that is worshipped; so that he as God sitteth in the temple of God, shewing himself that he is God. 5 Remember ye not, that, when I was yet with you, I told you these things?*

Mark 14:17-21 *And in the evening he cometh with the twelve. 18 And as they sat and did eat, Jesus said, Verily I say unto you, One of you which eateth with me shall betray me. 19 And they began to be sorrowful, and to say unto him one by one, Is it I? and another said, Is it I? 20 And he answered and said unto them, It is one of the twelve, that dippeth with me in the dish. 21 The Son of man indeed goeth, as it is written of him: but woe to that man by whom the Son of man is betrayed!* **good were it for that man if he had never been born.**

Luke 22:3 *Then entered Satan into Judas surnamed Iscariot, being of the number of the twelve.*

But the bad news on Judas does not stop here- Consider what Apostle Peter and King David say about Judas Iscariot. *Psalm 109* details prophecy concerning Judas Iscariot- in much the same way *Psalm 22* does about Jesus Christ. Consider also when Judas died, scripture says he went *to his own place.* Apostle Peter quotes from Psalms.

Acts 1:15-20 *And in those days Peter stood up in the midst of the disciples, and said, (the number of names together were about an hundred and twenty,)* **16 Men and brethren, this scripture must needs have been fulfilled, which the Holy Ghost by the mouth of David spake**

before concerning Judas, which was guide to them that took Jesus. *17* For he was numbered with us, and had obtained part of this ministry. *18* Now this man purchased a field with the reward of iniquity; and falling headlong, he burst asunder in the midst, and all his bowels gushed out. *19* And it was known unto all the dwellers at Jerusalem; insomuch as that field is called in their proper tongue, Aceldama, that is to say, The field of blood. **20 For it is written in the book of Psalms, Let his habitation be desolate, and let no man dwell therein: and his bishoprick let another take.**

Acts 1:25 That he may take part of this ministry and apostleship, from which Judas by transgression fell, **that he might go to his own place.**

Psalms 109:6-9 Set thou a wicked man over him: and let Satan stand at his right hand. *7* When he shall be judged, let him be condemned: and let his prayer become sin. *8* Let his days be few; and let another take his office.

In the book of Revelation, an angel gives Apostle John information concerning the Antichrist (also called the beast.) Notice the link to perdition. So how do we interpret, *the beast was and is not and yet is ?*

During Jesus Christ ministry, Judas was alive so **he was-**
At the time John wrote Revelation, Judas was dead- so **he was not**
During the Tribulation period Judas is here again so- **he yet is**

Revelation 17:7-8 And the angel said unto me, Wherefore didst thou marvel? I will tell thee the mystery of the woman, and of the beast that carrieth her, which hath the seven heads and ten horns. **8 The beast that thou sawest was, and is not; and shall ascend out of the bottomless pit, and go into perdition:** and they that dwell on the earth shall wonder, whose names were not written in the book of life from the foundation of the world, when they behold **the beast that was, and is not, and yet is.**

THOUGHT TO PONDER

Judas never called Jesus Lord; he called him master. Every time the Bible provides a list of the Apostles, Peter is named first and Judas is named last: *Matthew 10:2-4; Mark 3:14-19; Luke 6:13-16.*

Mystery of Iniquity

§

*2 THESSALONIANS 2:7-10 FOR THE **mystery of iniquity** doth already work: only he who now letteth will let, until he be taken out of the way. **8** And then shall that Wicked be revealed, whom the Lord shall consume with the spirit of his mouth, and shall destroy with the brightness of his coming: **9** Even him, whose coming is after the working of Satan with all power and signs and lying wonders,*

*   **1 Timothy 3:16** And without controversy great is **the mystery of godliness**: God was manifest in the flesh, justified in the Spirit, seen of angels, preached unto the Gentiles, believed on in the world, received up into glory.*

The mystery of godliness consists of a holy trinity: God the Father, God the Son, God the Holy Ghost. The mystery of iniquity consists of an unholy trinity: Satan the Dragon, Antichrist the son, and the False Prophet. Thus Satan, in an attempt to be like God, manifests himself in three beings: The satanic trinity stands in antitype or direct opposition to God. This does not mean Satan has equal power or equal ability as God. The Lord God is omniscient, omnipresent, and omnipotent; Satan possesses none of those qualities; however, he imitates them all. Satan is a created being. A revelation of the satanic trinity is revealed in Revelation chapter 13.

God the Father's---antitype is Leviathan
Jesus Christ's --- antitype is Antichrist
God the Holy Ghost---antitype is the False Prophet

During the final dispensation before Jesus' 2nd Coming, Antichrist rules the world. This period is referred to as Daniel's 70th Week. God calls the final 42 months of Daniel's 70th week the Great Tribulation.

The Antichrist (also called the beast) does not rule without help. Satan provides a religious counterpart called the False Prophet. Just as the Holy Ghost convinces people to worship Jesus, the False Prophet convinces mankind to worship Antichrist. Satan, also called the Dragon/ Leviathan, gives him power to work miracles and mighty wonders. Together, the Dragon, Antichrist, and the False Prophet form a satanic trinity. Although the satanic trinity has existed for thousands of years, its power climaxes during the Great Tribulation. People worship the Dragon; and they worship Antichrist on earth, while the False Prophet inspires and motivates worship.

Technology, especially wireless internet plays a huge role in giving the illusion Satan is omnipresent. The false prophet is the ultimate tech wizard. Satan's many titles include the prince of the powers of the air. As electrical technology advances, more and more atmospheric powers will be harnessed. All things in the physical world represent spiritual truth and the computer itself is a type of god as Satan attempts to manifest attributes of God-as one stares directly at an image.

COMPUTERS GIVE THE ILLUSION OF BEING A GOD.

1. Omniscient- through search engines and god-like memory.
2. Omnipresent- through internet and camera and imaging capacity.

3. Omnipotent- Computerized god like mathematical ability as the operator controls world economies and armies.

*Ephesians 2:2 Wherein in time past ye walked according to the course of this world, according to **the prince of the power of the air**, the spirit that now worketh in the children of disobedience:*

*Revelation 13:4 And they worshipped the **dragon** which gave power unto the beast: and they worshipped the **beast,** saying, Who is like unto the beast? who is able to make war with him?*

*Revelation 13:11-12 And I beheld **another beast** coming up out of the earth; and he had two horns like a lamb, and he spake as a dragon. 12 And he exerciseth all the power of the first beast before him, and causeth the earth and them which dwell therein to worship the first beast, **whose deadly wound was healed**.*

Antichrist takes total control of the world's economic systems, and thereby rules mankind. The Antichrist erects an image and the false prophet makes it come alive. The False Prophet also compels mankind to worship the beast and his image; anyone refusing to obey suffers death. Up until this point, the beast appears to help Israel, now he is their greatest enemy.

Revelation 13:13-15 And he doeth great wonders, so that he maketh fire come down from heaven on the earth in the sight of men, 14 And deceiveth them that dwell on the earth by the means of those miracles which he had power to do in the sight of the beast; saying to them that dwell on the earth, that they should make an image to the beast, which had the wound by a sword, and did live. 15 And he had power to give life unto the image of the beast, that the image of the beast should both speak, and cause that as many as would not worship the image of the beast should be killed.

Sometime during Antichrist's reign, he is killed and comes back to life. Notice in verse 12 the statement *whose deadly wound was healed*. Either an actual assassination or masterful deception takes place.

Spiritually, however, the devil imitates Jesus' death and resurrection. Remember he is the Antichrist. The beast imitates Christ in many ways. His resurrection, no doubt, causes religious jubilation. The world's savior was dead, but he lives again. During the terrible years that follow billions of people are killed, including 2/3 of the Jewish population. One positive result of the Great Tribulation is all Israel finally believes Jesus Christ is their Messiah.

Final judgment on satanic trinity

Revelation 19:20 *And the beast was taken, and with him the false prophet that wrought miracles before him, with which he deceived them that had received the mark of the beast, and them that worshipped his image. These both were cast alive into a lake of fire burning with brimstone.*

Revelation 20:10 *And the **devil** that deceived them was cast into the lake of fire and brimstone, where the **beast** and the **false prophet** are, and shall be tormented day and night for ever and ever.*

Daniel's Fourth Kingdom

America is in Prophecy

DEDICATION

THIS STUDY IS DEDICATED TO my Lord and Saviour, Jesus Christ. And to his Bride, may she be encouraged to pray, study, and work until the Bridegroom gathers us together. And to the believers who come after:

Deuteronomy 4:30-31 When thou art in tribulation, and all these things are come upon thee, even in the latter days, if thou turn to the LORD thy God, and shalt be obedient unto his voice; 31 (For the LORD thy God is a merciful God;) he will not forsake thee, neither destroy thee, nor forget the covenant of thy fathers which he sware unto them.

Jeremiah 30:7 Alas! for that day is great, so that none is like it: it is even the time of Jacob's trouble; but he shall be saved out of it.

The Last Superpower

§

DANIEL 2:40 AND THE FOURTH kingdom shall be strong as iron: forasmuch as iron breaketh in pieces and subdueth all things: and as iron that breaketh all these, shall it break in pieces and bruise.

DANIEL IDENTIFIES THE FINAL WORLD SUPERPOWER AS THE FOURTH KINGDOM

If we are living in the last days, Daniel's Fourth Kingdom is upon us; one condition cannot exist without the other. The world's last great gentile empire is described with startling detail, its people, its character, its strengths, and sins. The Fourth Kingdom is a nation whose military power and political environment provides the means for a coming genius to rule the world. For any country (now or in the future) to name itself the Fourth Kingdom is unlikely; therefore, Bible students, living in the end times, will have to identify the nation's political name.

Last days' prophecies circle Israel as certainly as the moon orbits the earth. No enemy of Israel speaks of Jerusalem or Jews without including America in their conversation; how then can American Christians excuse themselves from the discussion? Ever cognizant that no scripture is of private interpretation and all interpretation of scripture is subject to the authority of God's word, this study is presented for consideration.

Present day America is transforming into the final phase of Daniel's Fourth Kingdom. America is evolving politically, morally, and socially, into something unrecognizable to the way the country was even 20 years ago. The unstoppable metamorphosis is well underway.

Daniel 7:23-25 *Thus he said,* **The fourth beast shall be the fourth kingdom** *upon earth, which shall be diverse from all kingdoms, and shall devour the whole earth, and shall tread it down, and break it in pieces.* ***24*** *And the ten horns out of this kingdom are ten kings that shall arise: and another shall rise after them; and he shall be diverse from the first, and he shall subdue three kings.* ***25*** *And he shall speak great words against the most High, and shall wear out the saints of the most High, and think to change times and laws: and they shall be given into his hand until a time and times and the dividing of time.*

Daniel describes the final condition of the Fourth Kingdom as a beast. It implements a global governing system dividing the world into ten political regions. Ten governors lead these territories while remaining subservient to the Fourth Kingdom. America exists in one of those regions in dominant hegemony form, exercising world economic control largely through the abilities of one individual. The army, marines, air force, and navy, gives the beast its iron teeth. Imagine a United Nations with the political and physical muscle to enforce its decrees.

After the new global government is in place, the Antichrist appears. He establishes himself dictator with ten subordinate kings. Insatiably opposed to God's righteousness, Antichrist changes laws and legislates sin. Knowing God destroys Babylon (the most powerful influential city on earth); Antichrist moves his seat of power to Jerusalem. Quite possibly, the United Nations moves to Jerusalem years before this happens. Such a move seeks to calm a hysterically violent Middle East, and appears conciliatory to Americans who want the UN out of New York. In reality, the move facilitates the coming abomination of desolation by giving Antichrist access to a rebuilt Jerusalem temple.

2 Peter 1:20 Knowing this first, that no prophecy of the scripture is of any private interpretation.

Psalms 119:18 Open thou mine eyes, that I may behold wondrous things out of thy law.

Gentile Kingdoms

§

DANIEL SUMMARIZES THE HISTORY OF world governments in a simple and understandable manner. The Book of Daniel also provides the foundation for this Bible study. The reader should read Daniel chapter two carefully.

PARAPHRASE AND SUMMARY DANIEL CHAPTER TWO.

In 500 BC the dominant gentile kingdom was Babylon. King Nebuchadnezzar was on the throne. One night Nebuchadnezzar dreams a very upsetting dream; consequently, he calls an emergency governmental session. He orders his wise men to tell him what his dream meant. In those days the Babylonian leaders were astrologers, magicians, sorcerers, and Chaldeans. (*Imagine an American president having a nightmare and then ordering Congress and the Senate into an emergency session to discuss his dream. As ridiculous as this sounds, that is basically what happened*)   below a paraphrase of the episode:

King Nebuchadnezzar to his wise men, "I've had a terrible dream, and I know it means something, but I'm not sure what it is. You have to help me with it."

"Sure we can help you," said the wise men, "tells us your dream and we'll give you the interpretation."

"That's part of the problem," says Nebuchadnezzar, "I have forgotten my dream. All I know now is I'm upset about it. You guys tell me what I dreamed, and then you tell me the interpretation."

"That's completely unreasonable," protest the wise men.

"That's the way it goes," says the king. "And if you don't tell me, I am going to kill you. And then I'm confiscating all your houses and turning them into public bathrooms and landfills."

"Nobody on earth can do what you ask," complain the wise men. "Your request is outrageous!"

"Tough, I'm King and that's the deal. I don't trust you guys anyway."

The top police and military people were called, and preparations began to start executing all the wise men. Fortunately, a young man named Daniel steps forward and says, "Hold on, there- don't kill anybody. Just calm down for a moment, and I will pray and ask God to show me the king's dream. And then I'll tell him the interpretation."

So Daniel, a young Israeli slave, held a prayer meeting with his closest buddies; and God told Daniel Nebuchadnezzar's dream. Daniel then informed the police he could answer all the king's questions. Next the police rushed Daniel to the king.

"So do you really know what's going on in my dream?" asks King Nebuchadnezzar.

"God told me," says Daniel. "My God knows everything."

"Well let's hear it then," says the king.

"In your dream you saw a great image of a man composed of various metals. The metals degenerated in value, starting with gold and ending with iron mixed with clay. It was really scary looking. The man's head was gold, his arms and breast silver, his stomach and thighs brass, and his legs and feet were iron- the feet actually mixed with clay and iron. Then a huge stone came crashing down from the sky and smashed the image of the man into pieces."

Daniel 2:31-34 Thou, O king, sawest, and behold a great image. This great image, whose brightness was excellent, stood before thee; and the form thereof was terrible. 32 This image's head was of fine gold, his breast and his arms of silver, his belly and his thighs of brass, 33 His legs of iron, his feet part of iron and part of clay. 34 Thou sawest till that a stone was cut out without hands, which smote the image upon his feet that were of iron and clay, and brake them to pieces.

"That's amazing, says Nebuchadnezzar, "That is exactly what I saw. Now what's it all mean?"

"God showed you the future of the world," continued Daniel. "In regards to major kingdoms, those different metals and human body parts represent the different future kingdoms. The head of gold represents you, King Nebuchadnezzar, and the Babylonian Kingdom. The kingdom coming next represented by the silver arms and breast. Then after them comes a 3rd kingdom represented by the brass loins and thighs. And then the iron legs and feet is the final 4th kingdom. And at the end of the 4th kingdom the ten toes are mixed up with clay."

*Daniel 2:38-40 And wheresoever the children of men dwell, the beasts of the field and the fowls of the heaven hath he given into thine hand, and hath made thee ruler over them all. **Thou art this head of gold.** 39 And after thee shall arise another kingdom inferior to thee, and another third kingdom of brass, which shall bear rule over all the earth. 40 And the fourth kingdom shall be strong as iron: forasmuch as iron breaketh in pieces and subdueth all things: and as iron that breaketh all these, shall it break in pieces and bruise.*

Daniel 2:41-45 And whereas thou sawest the feet and toes, part of potters' clay, and part of iron, the kingdom shall be divided; but there shall be in it of the strength of the iron, forasmuch as thou sawest the iron mixed with miry clay. 42 And as the toes of the feet were part of iron, and part of clay, so the kingdom shall be partly strong, and partly broken. 43 And whereas thou sawest iron mixed with miry clay, they shall mingle themselves with the seed of men: but they shall not cleave one to another, even as iron is not mixed with clay. **44** *And in the days of these kings shall the God of heaven set up a kingdom, which shall never be destroyed: and the kingdom shall not be left to other people, but it shall break in pieces and consume all these kingdoms, and it shall stand for ever.* **45** *Forasmuch as thou sawest that the stone was cut out of the mountain without hands, and that it brake in pieces the iron, the brass, the clay, the silver, and the gold; the great God hath made known to the king what shall come to pass hereafter: and the dream is certain, and the interpretation thereof sure.*

"That's terrific," says Nebuchadnezzar, "I'm making you my top advisor.

Paraphrase end

History records the world kingdoms represented by Nebuchadnezzar's image as: Head of Gold, Babylon. Silver chest and arms depicted the jointly ruling Medes and Persians, followed by Brass Grecian Empire, and then Iron Roman reaching down through the ages till the end of days. Many able writers and historians discuss them at great length. This study is basically involved with events pertaining to the final phase (era) of the Fourth Kingdom, the feet and toes of the image.

Historical Foundations

MUCH OF THE BIBLE IS an accounting of Israel's history. The Israeli nation may be viewed as God's time-piece (or time bomb), both metaphors are accurate. Opinions concerning Israel are vast and diverse, from devout love to seething hatred, and every level of feeling in between. Yet prophecies regarding Israel prove the Bible knows the future. Personal, political, or religious feelings have nothing to do with the historical evidence.

Thought to ponder: America's relationship with Israel is very curious. America has been a solid ally to Israel ever since President Truman acknowledged Israel's rebirth eleven minutes after David Ben Gurion declared it, May 14, 1948. Although America does not have biblical proof that God founded the USA (as he did Israel) but a large number of Americans consider their nation birthed by God. In the author's opinion America's success, blessings, and current mercies are due to the fact America supports Israel. Full depth and understanding of the Israeli American connection may not be realized until heaven. The heart of Jer**usa**lem may be more than letters, but thankfully, America has stood with Israel with blood and treasure since God reinstated the Jews back in their land. The last days' countdown commenced May 14, 1948.

Genesis 12:3 *And I will bless them that bless thee, and curse him that curseth thee: and in thee shall all families of the earth be blessed.*

Several prophecies identify the times in which we live as the last days. But are prophecies truly on the level? Or are they so obscure and vague that private interpretation relates these predictions to almost any incident? This study correlates significant current events with specific biblical prophecy. The only interpretation the reader should be concerned with is his/her own. Words mean what they say; the Bible proves itself.

Numerous prophecies concern events just prior to the Second Coming of Jesus Christ. The Bible verses in this article are a minimum of 1,900 years old, the New Testament written in the first century AD. The Old Testament is much older.

Understanding prophecy necessitates some basic knowledge of Israel's history. Around 2,000 BC, God founded Israel under the patriarch Abram. Later Abram's name changed to Abraham.

Genesis 12:1-3 *Now the LORD had said unto Abram, Get thee out of thy country, and from thy kindred, and from thy father's house, unto a land that I will shew thee: **2** And I will make of thee a great nation, and I will bless thee, and make thy name great; and thou shalt be a blessing: **3** And I will bless them that bless thee, and curse him that curseth thee: and in thee shall all families of the earth be blessed.*

Abraham had a son named Isaac. Isaac had a son named Jacob; God changed Jacob's name to Israel. Jacob's twelve sons became the twelve tribes of Israel. In fact, the name of those twelve sons, designate the twelve tribes of Israel. Jacob and his sons immigrate to Egypt. Over several centuries they multiplied to around 3,000,000 people.

Eventually the Jews became slaves to the Egyptians, and God used a leader named Moses to deliver them out of Egypt. (1491 BC) Moses directed the Israelites to their promised land. Over the next several hundred years, Israel developed into a significant nation. But Israel's standing in the world remained contingent on her relationship with the Lord. God warned Israel over and over, (throughout the centuries) if they did not repent and serve Him, he would dissolve their nation and scatter them around the world. The Bible verses below explain God's intentions quite clearly.

*Deuteronomy 28:63-65 And it shall come to pass, that as the LORD rejoiced over you to do you good, and to multiply you; so the LORD will rejoice over you to destroy you, and to bring you to nought; and ye shall be plucked from off the land whither thou goest to possess it. **64 And the LORD shall scatter thee among all people, from the one end of the earth even unto the other;** and there thou shalt serve other gods, which neither thou nor thy fathers have known, even wood and stone. **65** And among these nations shalt thou find no ease, neither shall the sole of thy foot have rest: but the LORD shall give thee there a trembling heart, and failing of eyes, and sorrow of mind:*

*Amos 9:8-9 Behold, the eyes of the Lord GOD are upon the sinful kingdom, and I will destroy it from off the face of the earth; saving that **I will not utterly destroy the house of Jacob, saith the LORD.** 9 For, lo, I will command, and I will sift the house of Israel among all nations, like as corn is sifted in a sieve, yet shall not the least grain fall upon the earth.*

Deuteronomy 4:27 And the LORD shall scatter you among the nations, and ye shall be left few in number among the heathen, whither the LORD shall lead you.

About 1,000 years after Moses, Israel had become a moral and spiritual disaster. God followed through on his warnings and dissolved Israel as a nation, the Jews scattered and taken captive by their enemies. This scattering (or the Diaspora) actually happened twice in history. Around 600 BC, God used the Gentile nations Assyria and Babylon to invade and conquer Israel, scattering the Jews throughout the Mesopotamian region. Nebuchadnezzar, king of Babylon, sacked Jerusalem and burned the temple to the ground. He took a remnant of surviving Jews, as captives, back to Babylon. Seventy years later, the Jews returned to Israel and rebuilt their temple. In the verse below, we learn the prophet Jeremiah predicted the seventy-year captivity in Babylon, and the Jews eventually return to their land.

Jeremiah 29:10 For thus saith the LORD, That after seventy years be accomplished at Babylon I will visit you, and perform my good word toward you, in causing you to return to this place.

Fast forward to 30 AD, about 400 years after the Jews returned to Israel –In New Testament times Jesus was on the scene. Israel's second and most significant scattering came about 35 years after the death and resurrection of Jesus Christ. In great sorrow, Jesus spoke these prophetic words over Jerusalem.

*Luke 19:41-44 And when he was come near, he beheld the city, and wept over it, 42 Saying, If thou hadst known, even thou, at least in this thy day, the things which belong unto thy peace! but now they are hid from thine eyes. 43 For the days shall come upon thee, that thine enemies shall cast a trench about thee, and compass thee round, and keep thee in on every side, 44 And shall lay thee even with the ground, and thy children within thee; and **they shall not leave in thee one stone upon another; because thou knewest not the time of thy visitation.***

*Luke 21:23-24 But woe unto them that are with child, and to them that give suck, in those days! for there shall be great distress in the land, and wrath upon this people. 24 And they shall fall by the edge of the sword, **and shall be led away captive into all nations: and Jerusalem shall be trodden down of the Gentiles, until the times of the Gentiles be fulfilled.***

*Matthew 24:2 And Jesus said unto them, See ye not all these things? verily I say unto you, There shall **not be left here one stone upon another, that shall not be thrown down.***

About 30 years after Jesus' resurrection, a great political re-bellion took place in Jerusalem. Rome, fed up with trouble in the Middle East, especially with Israel, Emperor Vespasian commanded his army to destroy Jerusalem. The temple literally dismantled stone by stone, an exact fulfillment of prophecy, see *Matthew 24:2*. And by the year 135 AD, Israel was off the map, the country no longer even recognized by its biblical name. In a futile effort to eradicate Jewish nationalism, the world referred to Israel's land as Palestine, and so it remained until 1948.

Second Return

§

Israel, as a political state, did not exist between the years 135 AD and 1948 AD. Ironically, Adolph Hitler's attempt to exterminate the Jew ultimately resulted in the state of Israel. On May 14, 1948 the state of Israel came back into existence. Isaiah, a prophet around 700 BC, gives more details on this re-gathering of Jews. Remember, God dissolved Israel once before when Assyria and Babylon conquered Israel.

*Isaiah 11:11-12 And it shall come to pass in that day, that the Lord shall set his hand **again the second time to recover the remnant of his people,** which shall be left, from Assyria, and from Egypt, and from Pathros, and from Cush, and from Elam, and from Shinar, and from Hamath, and from the islands of the sea. 12 And he shall set up an ensign for the nations, and shall assemble the outcasts of Israel, and gather together the dispersed of Judah from the four corners of the earth.*

Notice the prophecy discusses the second time God re-gathers his people. This statement by Isaiah fulfilled literally in 1948. The first time God returned the Jew to Israel came after the Babylonian captivity around 500 BC. The second time was after nearly 1,900 years of exile. For a people to exist with national identity after nearly 2 millennia without geographic borders or organized government defies all logic and reason. Only a miracle kept Israel a segregated people. Why weren't the Jews assimilated into the various nations and cultures where the Lord scattered them? There is only one answer- God kept them together. Remarkably, Isaiah made the "second time" prophecy before the Jews left their homeland for the first time.

The Bible plainly says Israel exists and is populated by Jews before Jesus returns. **The return of the Jews to Israel was a scriptural requirement.** Because the Jews rejected their messiah, God dissolved the nation, and he scattered the Jews around the whole world. But not forever! Many times the Bible discusses God's anger with the Jews and the scattering of Israel, but there is always a promise of restoring the nation.

Deuteronomy 30:1-6 And it shall come to pass, when all these things are come upon thee, the blessing and the curse, which I have set before thee, and thou shalt call them to mind among all the nations, whither the LORD thy God hath driven thee, 2 And shalt return unto the LORD thy God, and shalt obey his voice according to all that I command thee this day, thou and thy children, with all thine heart, and with all thy soul; **3 That then the LORD thy God will turn thy captivity, and have compassion upon thee, and will return and gather thee from all the nations, whither the LORD thy God hath scattered thee.** *4 If any of thine be driven out unto the outmost parts of heaven, from thence will the LORD thy God gather thee, and from thence will he fetch thee:* **5 And the LORD thy God will bring thee into the land which thy fathers possessed, and thou shalt possess it; and he will do thee good, and multiply thee above thy fathers.** *6 And the LORD thy God will circumcise thine heart, and the heart of thy seed, to love the LORD thy God with all thine heart, and with all thy soul, that thou mayest live.*

Jews Return Unconverted

§

CAREFUL READING REVEALS THE JEWS must return to Israel in an unconverted spiritual condition; a significant prophetic point. The Jews turn to God after they are in their land. Present day Israelis do not accept Jesus Christ as their Messiah, but they soon will.

When I was a young, children sometimes sang a little song. *The foot bone connected to the anklebone, and the anklebone connected to the leg bone, the leg bone is connected to the hipbone etc.* The inspiration behind that little jingle is Prophet Ezekiel's vision of the valley of dry bones. The prophet witnessed a vision of bones joining back together, and then skin covering the bones. Ezekiel 37 predicts Israel getting back together as a nation, and then accepting the Lord as their Saviour.

*Ezekiel 37:1-4 The hand of the LORD was upon me, and carried me out in the spirit of the LORD, and set me down in the midst of the valley **which was full of bones,** 2 And caused me to pass by them round about: and, behold, there were very many in the open valley; and, lo, they were very dry. 3 And he said unto me, Son of man, can these bones live? And I answered, O Lord GOD, thou knowest. 4 Again he said unto me, Prophesy upon these bones, and say unto them, O ye dry bones, hear the word of the LORD.*

Whenever possible let the Bible interpret itself. For example, someone may be asking, "What are these bones? And what is Ezekiel talking about?" Verse 11 answers the question.

*Ezekiel 37:11-12 Then he said unto me, Son of man, **these bones are the whole house of Israel:** behold, they say, Our bones are dried, and our hope is lost: we are cut off for our parts. **12** Therefore prophesy and say unto them, Thus saith the Lord GOD; Behold, O my people, **I will open your graves**, and cause you to come up out of your graves, and bring you into the land of Israel.*

The Bible tells us the bones represent the whole house of Israel. This chapter is more difficult than previous texts, and requires some interpretation, but by proceeding logically, and letting scripture interpret scripture truth is realized. Also, we build on knowledge already learned about the Jews being scattered.

The graves depict the Gentile nations where God scattered the Jews. Notice the bones come together, and sinews and flesh are put on- and they return to the land of Israel; but the body is not breathing. The body has no spiritual life.

*Ezekiel 37:7-8 So I prophesied as I was commanded: and as I prophesied, there was a **noise, and behold a shaking,** and the bones came together, bone to his bone. **8** And when I beheld, lo, the sinews and the flesh came up upon them, and the skin covered them above: **but there was no breath in them.***

Remember the body represents the nation of Israel. So the nation is intact just before it comes to spiritual life. God presents us with an analogy, a perfectly reasonable way to communicate. Breath causes a body to live. And until a person, (any person Jew or Gentile) accepts Jesus Christ as LORD, they are considered spiritually dead. Observe before the bones come back together, a noise and a shaking happens. This event takes place just before the nation of Israel comes back into existence. In my opinion, the noise and shaking was World War Two, the war basically forced Israel into existence.

Ezekiel 37:6 *And I will lay sinews upon you, and will bring up flesh upon you, and cover you with skin, and put breath in you, and ye shall live; and ye shall know that I am the LORD.*

Summary

Prophets predicted Israel's dispersion throughout the Middle East hundreds of years prior to the actual event. These scatterings are referred to as Diasporas. The first scattering happened around 600 BC when Babylon conquered Israel and took a remnant captive to Babylon. The second Diaspora happened around 70 AD and lasted until 1948 AD.

* Prophets predict the nation Israel to be conquered, temple destroyed, and the people dispersed throughout the Gentile nations.
* Prophets predict Israel returns to the land and rebuild the temple. Fulfilled around 500 BC.
* Prophets and Jesus prophesy Israel endures a second Diaspora (scattering). This happened 70 AD- 135 AD-1948.
* Prophet Isaiah prophesizes Israel returns to their land in an unconverted spiritual condition. Fulfilled 1948
* Prophets predict Jerusalem returns to Israel. Fulfilled 1967
* Jews predicted to receive Messiah Jesus in their own land. This prophecy awaits fulfillment.

Zechariah 12:10 *And I will pour upon the house of David, and upon the inhabitants of Jerusalem, the spirit of grace and of supplications: and they shall look upon me whom they have pierced, and they shall mourn for* *him, as one mourneth for his only son, and shall be in bitterness for him, as one that is in bitterness for his firstborn.*

Romans 11:25-29 *For I would not, brethren, that ye should be ignorant of this mystery, lest ye should be wise in your own conceits; that blindness in part is happened to Israel, until the fulness of the Gentiles be come in. **26** And so all Israel shall be saved: as it is written, There shall come out of Sion the Deliverer, and shall turn away ungodliness from Jacob: **27** For this is my covenant unto them, when I shall take away their sins. **28** As concerning the gospel, they are enemies for your sakes: but as touching the election, they are beloved for the fathers' sakes. **29** For the gifts and calling of God are without repentance.*

Burdensome Stone

Jerusalem

WHAT BRINGING UP THE DEITY of Jesus Christ does to an ecumenical discussion on religion, Jerusalem does to a discussion about world politics.

Although Israel returned to their land in 1948, much of Jerusalem was not under Jewish control. This is very important because Jerusalem has its own prophetic significance. It took another war to get Jerusalem; which fulfilled another prophecy. This happened in 1967, remembered historically as the Six Day War.

In 1948, the United Nations and world consensus (except Islamic nations) favored Israel becoming a nation. But not one nation supports the Jews controlling Jerusalem. United Nations Resolution 242 documents this unhappy truth, which basically asserts Jerusalem belongs to the Arabs. And not even the United States officially disputes the document. Prophetically hugely important, because Jerusalem provokes the world's final war. Jerusalem specifically upsets the world. Consider Zechariah's preciseness. It's as though the prophet had a current newspaper.

Zechariah 12:1-3 *The burden of the word of the LORD for Israel, saith the LORD, which stretcheth forth the heavens, and layeth the foundation of the earth, and formeth the spirit of man within him.* ***2 Behold, I***

will make Jerusalem a cup of trembling unto all the people round about, *when they shall be in the siege both against Judah and against Jerusalem. 3 And in that day will **I make Jerusalem a burdensome stone for all people:** all that burden themselves with it shall be cut in pieces, though all the people of the earth be gathered together against it.*

*Zechariah 12:9-10 And it shall come to pass in that day, that **I will seek to destroy all the nations that come against Jerusalem.** 10 And I will pour upon the house of David, and upon the inhabitants of Jerusalem, the spirit of grace and of supplications: and they shall look upon me whom they have pierced, and they shall mourn for him, as one mourneth for his only son, and shall be in bitterness for him, as one that is in bitterness for his firstborn.*

Stop and think about Zechariah's prophecies. In 500 BC the whole world cared less about Jerusalem. To predict Jerusalem causes global war sounded absurd. But today, even the politically naive realize Jerusalem is a major source of trouble. In 500 BC, the technology to bring all of earth's nations to Jerusalem did not exist. Concentrating the whole world's armies requires sophisticated and massive transportation systems. National armies need ships and airplanes and even railroads to move them.

What makes Jerusalem so important anyway? The city provides religious significance for Christianity, Judaism, and Islam; but how did it ever get important enough to provoke World War? Israel is now surrounded by nations vowing to destroy her. And Israel openly threatens to use all power necessary to defend itself. Do not forget the Jew was also at the center of World War 2. Once again, an unexplainable situation, unless the Bible is consulted.

Why Jerusalem Provokes War

§

LOCATION, LOCATION, LOCATION

The answer to the Jerusalem question is spiritual, political, and prophetic. In the Millennium and eternity, God makes Jerusalem the capital of the earth. Jerusalem is also the capital of the universe, the exact place God puts His Temple and His throne. This overt biblical fact causes Satan to want his own throne in Jerusalem. Since Jesus Christ rules the kingdom of heaven (the whole universe) from Jerusalem, Satan is concentrating forces to try and stop it. In the years just before Jesus 2nd Advent, the Antichrist builds a temple in Jerusalem and places his own throne inside. Satan mocks and imitates God every chance he can.

SATAN'S LIE AND IMPERSONATION OF CHRIST

2 Thessalonians 2:3-5 Let no man deceive you by any means: for that day shall not come, except there come a falling away first, and that man of sin be revealed, the son of perdition; 4 Who opposeth and exalteth himself above all that is called God, or that is worshipped; so that he as God sitteth in the temple of God, shewing himself that he is God. 5 Remember ye not, that, when I was yet with you, I told you these things?

THE TRUE GOD RULES HEAVEN FROM JERUSALEM

Ezekiel 43:7 *And he said unto me,* **Son of man, the place of my throne, and the place of the soles of my feet, where I will dwell in the midst of the children of Israel for ever,** *and my holy name, shall the house of Israel no more defile, neither they, nor their kings, by their whoredom, nor by the carcases of their kings in their high places.*

Isaiah 2:1-3 *The word that Isaiah the son of Amoz saw concerning Judah and Jerusalem. 2 And it shall come to pass in the last days, that* **the mountain of the LORD'S house shall be established in the top of the mountains, and shall be exalted above the hills; and all nations shall flow unto it.** *3 And many people shall go and say, Come ye, and let us go up to the mountain of the LORD, to the house of the God of Jacob; and he will teach us of his ways, and we will walk in his paths: for out of Zion shall go forth the law, and the word of the LORD from Jerusalem.*

Antichrist and Jerusalem

§

THE GREATEST WORLD LEADER IS coming. Scripture knows him by many names: Antichrist, the beast, the man of sin, and son of perdition. He generates so much political appeal the whole world listens and obeys his commands. Potentially, the United Nations already provides a framework for a world government. If the U.S. armed forces submits to the U. N. (As they did during the Iraqi invasion of Kuwait in 1991) the United Nations could control the world by enforcing all its resolutions, including Resolution 242. What would it take for a majority of Americans to allow the United Nations' to control the US military again?

Certainly a dominant world problem today is the economy. Western nations, including America walk an economic tightrope on the verge of collapse. Much of the world lives in poverty; whole continents in danger of starvation. The United Nations looks for a leader who can solve these problems. Soon the master economist of the ages appears and provides solutions to the world's economic and political woes.

Revelation 13:16-17 And he causeth all, both small and great, rich and poor, free and bond, to receive a mark in their right hand, or in their foreheads: 17 And that no man might buy or sell, save he that had the mark, or the name of the beast, or the number of his name.

The Antichrist completely changes the entire world's economic system. Think of him as the greatest economist who ever lives. The Antichrist assigns a number to every human being. If you don't have a number, you can't buy or sell anything. Americans already have a Social Security Number. Someday soon this number (or similar number) is implanted in the body. We have the technology now, injectable computer chips. This technology started as a means to identify dogs and cats. A computer scanner reads the area of the body where the chip is located and the animal's medical record, owner's address, manifests on a computer screen.

THINK! This prophecy is nearly 2,000 years old. The technology identifying every human being and track all economic transactions was not possible until just recently. It takes computers to do this! The Bible predicted a cashless economy, an electronic economic system. Today, it is not only possible; it is imminent. Think of the tax dollars the government loses by all the buying and selling not reported. Once cash goes away and all transactions are computerized, the government realizes billions in new tax dollars. No more *under the table* dealings of any kind. The gained tax revenue from the underground economy probably provides the final incentives to make paper currency obsolete.

Consider what the elimination of currency does to crime. Imagine buying drugs electronically through a computer as the government monitors all economic transactions. What about gambling and prostitution? Also, did you know germs and viruses transport via money? Cash is a threat to your health. Perhaps the most important reason to digitalize cash is counterfeiting. Photo technology is so superb; counterfeiting is no longer just for the big time criminal. The problem of counterfeiting is far, far bigger than most people realize.

The plan to eliminate cash is well under way. The vast majority of wealth is already digitalized. Home equities, stocks, bonds, and checking accounts, and debit cards exemplify electronic money. The little need still remaining for cash goes away when the government assigns everyone a world credit card, like a **Master Card**- (think about that name for a while) Of course, losing the card would be a disaster. The solution to this problem is simple. Implant the number under the skin. Then the person could never lose his mark, nor could his mark be stolen. *Revelation 13:16-17* - Notice God says the mark is "in their hand" or "in their forehead" The Bible's prediction for the mark is in a person- not on a person! This prophecy, alone, proves the Bible knows the future. Considering gained tax revenue, identity theft, fraud, counterfeiting, and spreading disease- going cashless is a practical and a good idea. The Bible simply said it happens- not why it happens.

As the Antichrist's success and genius becomes more and more obvious the world becomes mesmerized by his power. When he announces his deity, their political adoration turns to worship.

Revelation 13:8-9 And all that dwell upon the earth shall worship him, whose names are not written in the book of life of the Lamb slain from the foundation of the world. 9 If any man have an ear, let him hear.

The Jewish people convert to Jesus Christ before the Second Coming. But not before they go through some very tough times. The Jew, along with the rest of the world, initially accepts the Antichrist as a great leader. But when the Antichrist claims to be God, the Jew refuses to go along with Satan's agenda. At that time, Satan's primary goal seeks to exterminate the Jew.

2 Thessalonians 2:3-5 Let no man deceive you by any means: for that day shall not come, except there come a falling away first, and that man of sin be revealed, the son of perdition; 4 Who opposeth and exalteth himself above all that is called God, or that is worshipped; so that he as God sitteth in the temple of God, shewing himself that he is God. 5 Remember ye not, that, when I was yet with you, I told you these things?

Revelation 13:15 *And he had power to give life unto the image of the beast, that the image of the beast should both speak, and cause that as many as would not worship the image of the beast should be killed.*

In order for the Antichrist to sit in the temple, the temple must be rebuilt; another prophecy. Although the temple in Jerusalem is not built (as of 2003), serious efforts toward rebuilding are currently underway. The Antichrist may be the one who orders the temple rebuilt or it may already be built when he arrives. Two things are certain:

1. The temple gets rebuilt.
2. The Antichrist sits in it and claims to be God.

People who reject Jesus Christ today risk their eternal destiny. The Bible says the Antichrist appears with signs and lying wonders. Those signs and lying wonders remain to be seen. Just solving the world debt crisis might be enough? However Satan does it, his entrance onto the world scene impresses everyone.

Millions of people alive right now know the Bible isn't a fairy tale. They understand human writers did not invent salvation in Jesus Christ. They know Jesus died and rose again, and they should take Him to be their Saviour. But they still refuse to get saved. God's patience and long-suffering does not wait forever. And people who want nothing to do with the real Jesus Christ eventually believe Satan and his lies. God deludes their minds and causes them to believe the devil. If the reader is not a Christian, I urge you to ask Jesus to save you right now. With verses like you are about to read, it's very risky business putting off salvation.

2 Thessalonians 2:9-12 *Even him, whose coming is after the working of Satan with all power and signs and lying wonders, 10 And with all deceivableness of unrighteousness in them that perish; because they received not the love of the truth, that they might be saved. 11 And for this cause God shall send them strong delusion, that they should believe a lie: 12 That they all might be damned who believed not the truth, but had pleasure in unrighteousness.*

SUMMARY

1. After 2,000 years, Israel re-established statehood in 1948.
2. Jerusalem, 1967.
3. The Middle East/ Jerusalem escalates world problems.
4. A great world leader appears.
5. The Jewish temple is rebuilt in Jerusalem.
6. World war over Jerusalem.
7. Great religious leader appears. Rules with Antichrist.

Great Religious Leader

THE ANTICHRIST DOES NOT RULE without help. Satan provides a religious counterpart called the False Prophet. Just as the Holy Ghost convinces people to worship Jesus, the False Prophet convinces mankind to worship the Antichrist. Satan, also called the Dragon, gives him power to work miracles and mighty wonders. Together, the Dragon, Antichrist, and the False Prophet form a satanic trinity. Their miracles culminate at the temple in Jerusalem. An image of the Antichrist is erected and the false prophet makes it come alive. The False Prophet also commands mankind to worship the beast and his image. Anyone refusing is killed. Up until this point, the beast appears to help Israel, now he is their greatest enemy.

*Revelation 13:11-15 And I beheld another beast coming up out of the earth; and he had two horns like a lamb, and he spake as a dragon. **12** And he exerciseth all the power of the first beast before him, and causeth the earth and them which dwell therein to worship the first beast, **whose deadly wound was healed. 13** And he doeth great wonders, so that he maketh fire come down from heaven on the earth in the sight of men, **14** And deceiveth them that dwell on the earth by the means of those miracles which he had power to do in the sight of the beast; saying to them that dwell on the earth, that they should make an image to the beast, which had the wound by a sword, and did live. **15** And he had power to give life unto the* *image of the beast, that the image of the beast should both speak, and cause that as many as would not worship the image of the beast should be killed.*

Sometime during Antichrist's reign, he is killed and comes back to life. Notice in verse 12 the statement *whose deadly wound was healed.* Perhaps an assassination or a masterful deception? Spiritually, however, the devil imitates Jesus' death and resurrection. Remember he is Antichrist. The beast imitates Christ in many ways. His resurrection, no doubt, causes hysterical jubilation on the earth. The world's savior died, but he lives again. During the terrible years that follow 2/3 of the total Jewish population perish.

Zechariah 13:8-9 And it shall come to pass, that in all the land, saith the LORD, two parts therein shall be cut off and die; but the third shall be left therein. 9 And I will bring the third part through the fire, and will refine them as silver is refined, and will try them as gold is tried: they shall call on my name, and I will hear them: I will say, It is my people: and they shall say, The LORD is my God.

Millions of Gentiles also die from war, plagues, and unimaginable horrors (read Revelation chapter 9) Anyone, Jew or Gentile, refusing to take the number of the beast, is killed. Regarding the killing of Jews, specifically; Satan has tried to genocide the Jew several times in history. In the days of Moses, Pharaoh ordered the midwives to kill all male children. Had this order been obeyed, the Jew would not exist.

Exodus 1:15-16 And the king of Egypt spake to the Hebrew midwives, of which the name of the one was Shiphrah, and the name of the other Puah: 16 And he said, When ye do the office of a midwife to the Hebrew women, and see them upon the stools; if it be a son, then ye shall kill him: but if it be a daughter, then she shall live.

Then again in the days of the first Diaspora, King Ahasuerus ordered all Jews destroyed. The Jewish holiday, Purim, still celebrates the failure of that genocidal effort, recorded in the book of Esther.

***Esther 3:13** And the letters were sent by posts into all the king's provinces, to destroy, to kill, and to cause to perish, all Jews, both young and old, little children and women, in one day, even upon the thirteenth day of the twelfth month, which is the month Adar, and to take the spoil of them for a prey.*

Over the centuries, pogrom after pogrom took place throughout Europe. Hideous treatment of Jews during WW2 led many Christians to suspect Adolph Hitler was the Antichrist. But, Hitler was not the final Antichrist, because the state of Israel and the temple did not yet exist. The world's president rules from Jerusalem- not Germany.

Many prophecies concern the Jews in the Millennium. Satan knows all this and to make a long story short, if Satan could annihilate the Jew, he wins his war with God. Satan, of course, fails; but it logically explains the hatred of the Jew. Satan, the false prophet, and the beast all have their own dreaded prophecies awaiting them.

***Revelation 19:20** And the beast was taken, and with him the false prophet that wrought miracles before him, with which he deceived them that had received the mark of the beast, and them that worshipped his image. These both were cast alive into a lake of fire burning with brimstone.*

***Revelation 20:10** And the devil that deceived them was cast into the lake of fire and brimstone, where the beast and the false prophet are, and shall be tormented day and night for ever and ever.*

During the world's last seven years, the Antichrist and the false prophet rule. The Bible refers to this time as Daniel's 70th Week. During the last 42 months a great Tribulation erupts resulting in the death of billions. A designed result of the Tribulation is to convert the Jewish nation to Jesus Christ. God's relationship to Israel is a great mystery. Today we live in the last days of the *times of the Gentiles*. And these times are nearly fulfilled, *Luke 21:23-24.*

This present age is also called the Church Age. The Church consists of born again believers; it is not a specific denomination. Christians put their faith in Jesus Christ for salvation. In the Church Age, there is no difference between Jews and Gentiles. The vast majority of true believers over the last 2,000 years have been Gentiles; thus God refers to the Church Age as *times of the Gentiles.*

Apostle Paul wrote about Israel's mystery relationship to God and the Church.

Romans 11:25-28 *For I would not, brethren, that ye should be ignorant of this mystery, lest ye should be wise in your own conceits; that blindness in part is happened to Israel, until the fulness of the Gentiles be come in.* **26** *And so all Israel shall be saved: as it is written, There shall come out of Sion the Deliverer, and shall turn away ungodliness from Jacob:* **27** *For this is my covenant unto them, when I shall take away their sins.* **28** *As concerning the gospel, they are enemies for your sakes: but as touching the election, they are beloved for the fathers' sakes.*

Luke 21:24 *And they shall fall by the edge of the sword, and shall be led away captive into all nations: and Jerusalem shall be trodden down of the Gentiles, until the times of the Gentiles be fulfilled.*

THE RAPTURE OF THE CHURCH

The last generation of Christians do not die physically; God translates them into heaven in an instant. This evacuation is popularly called the rapture of the church. Literally, the Bible refers to the rapture as a resurrection. The bodies of deceased Christians resurrect first, and then a moment later the bodies of living Christians become immortal; Jesus gathers both groups together in the air.

THE RAPTURE IS A DISTINCT AND SEPARATE EVENT FROM THE 2ND COMING OF JESUS CHRIST. THE RAPTURE IS A GOING AWAY; IT IS NOT A RETURNING.

1 Thessalonians 4:13-18 But I would not have you to be ignorant, brethren, concerning them which are asleep, that ye sorrow not, even as others which have no hope. 14 For if we believe that Jesus died and rose again, even so them also which sleep in Jesus will God bring with him. 15 For this we say unto you by the word of the Lord, that we which are alive and remain unto the coming of the Lord shall not prevent them which are asleep. 16 For the Lord himself shall descend from heaven with a shout, with the voice of the archangel, and with the trump of God: and the dead in Christ shall rise first: 17 Then we which are alive and remain shall be caught up together with them in the clouds, to meet the Lord in the air: and so shall we ever be with the Lord. 18 Wherefore comfort one another with these words.

1 Corinthians 15:50-54 Now this I say, brethren, that flesh and blood cannot inherit the kingdom of God; neither doth corruption inherit incorruption. 51 Behold, I shew you a mystery; We shall not all sleep, but we shall all be changed, 52 In a moment, in the twinkling of an eye, at the last trump: for the trumpet shall sound, and the dead shall be raised incorruptible, and we shall be changed. 53 For this corruptible must put on incorruption, and this mortal must put on immortality. 54 So when this corruptible shall have put on incorruption, and this mortal shall have put on immortality, then shall be brought to pass the saying that is written, Death is swallowed up in victory.

Three Babylons

§

IDENTIFYING DANIEL'S FOURTH BEAST

BABYLON, MEANS *CONFUSION, OR TO confuse by mixing.*

Curiously, scripture highlights Babylon three times: in the beginning of the Bible, in the middle of the Bible, and in the end of the Bible. Examining similarities between these empires, helps identify the Fourth Kingdom. All three Babylonian empires include six dominant identifying characteristics:

1. Babylon is always a leading nation for trade, commerce, and political influence. Babylon is the world's main consumer of goods.
2. Biblical description of Babylon always includes a nation and a spectacular city.
3. The nucleus or majority of God's people live in Babylon during the height of its power.
4. Architecture. The Babylonian empire always obsessed with towers or tall buildings.
5. Military strength. Babylon is always the undisputed world super power.
6. Babylon is always ambitious toward becoming a one world government.

BABYLON EMPIRE NUMBER ONE, 2,247 BC

Geographically, the first Babylon was located in the world's middle-eastern region, known today as Iraq. This Babylonian empire was man's first kingdom after Noah's flood. Originally called Babel, it later came to be known as Babylon. Its founder's name, Nimrod, means *we will rebel*. The title, **Babylon, means *confusion, or to confuse by mixing.***

Genesis 10:8-10 *And Cush begat Nimrod: he began to be a mighty one in the earth.* **9** *He was a mighty hunter before the LORD: wherefore it is said, Even as Nimrod the mighty hunter before the LORD.* **10 *And the beginning of his kingdom was Babel,*** *and Erech, and Accad, and Calneh, in the land of Shinar.*

Often overlooked is the citizenry of Babel included men like Noah and Shem and anyone else who believed in the Lord. Even though the empire existed 100 years after the great flood, Noah still lived. Prophetically, this is hugely significant, because the *days of Noah* - included the first Babylonian empire. God's people lived in Babylon. Jesus referenced the days of Noah to his 2ⁿᵈ Coming. In other words, he implied things would be similar or like things were in the days of Noah.

Matthew 24:37 *But as the days of Noe were, so shall also the coming of the Son of man be.*

So when interpreting the *days of Noah* -remember to consider the 350 years Noah lived after the flood. The days of Noah included the formation of a one world government. Although Babylon's population was rather small, it represented efforts toward world government.

Most people know something about the Tower of Babel, the great high tower the people were building so they could reach heaven. Before Babylonians completed the magnificent tower, however, God stepped in confounding the language, and at the same time separated the earth's population. (And divided the earth's land)

Genesis 11:4-9 And they said, Go to, let us build us a city and a tower, whose top may reach unto heaven; and let us make us a name, lest we be scattered abroad upon the face of the whole earth. 5 And the LORD came down to see the city and the tower, which the children of men builded. 6 And the LORD said, Behold, the people is one, and they have all one language; and this they begin to do: and now nothing will be restrained from them, which they have imagined to do. 7 Go to, let us go down, and there confound their language, that they may not understand one another's speech. 8 So the LORD scattered them abroad from thence upon the face of all the earth: and they left off to build the city. 9 Therefore is the name of it called Babel; because the LORD did there confound the language of all the earth: and from thence did the LORD scatter them abroad upon the face of all the earth.

Babylon Empire Number Two   582 BC

After the Genesis account, Babylon shows up next in the middle of history. In 582 BC, Babylon, once again a thriving kingdom, enjoys world dominance. Like Babylon number one her geographic location is Iraq. As far as its military might and wealth, no country on earth could rival Babylon. The country's capital epitomizes the greatest city on earth. History records many accounts of the city's magnificent architectural structures. The city's walls reached 300 feet high and built wide enough for several chariots to ride side by side on the top. Numerous temples and buildings within the city loomed even taller than the walls. An ancient world wonder, Babylon's hanging gardens, grew on a fabricated mountain rising above the city like a colossal jewel. Truly this ancient metropolis represented magnificent human achievements.

God used Babylon's most famous king, Nebuchadnezzar, to bring judgment on a backsliding nation of Judah. The Babylonians attacked Jerusalem and burned the Jewish temple to the ground. The Jews were taken captive into Babylon; therefore, the largest population of believing Jews lived in Babylon. Like Babylon Number One, God's people were centered in Babylon. During the Babylonian Captivity Daniel wrote the great prophetic book of Daniel.

2 Chronicles 36:13-20 And he also rebelled against king Nebuchadnezzar, who had made him swear by God: but he stiffened his neck, and hardened his heart from turning unto the LORD God of Israel. 14 Moreover all the chief of the priests, and the people, transgressed very much after all the abominations of the heathen; and polluted the house of the LORD which he had hallowed in Jerusalem. 15 And the LORD God of their fathers sent to them by his messengers, rising up betimes, and sending; because he had compassion on his people, and on his dwelling place: 16 But they mocked the messengers of God, and despised his words, and misused his prophets, until the wrath of the LORD arose against his people, till there was no remedy. 17 Therefore he brought upon them the king of the Chaldees, who slew their young men with the sword in the house of their sanctuary, and had no compassion upon young man or maiden, old man, or him that stooped for age: he gave them all into his hand. 18 And all the vessels of the house of God, great and small, and the treasures of the house of the LORD, and the treasures of the king, and of his princes; all these he brought to Babylon. 19 And they burnt the house of God, and brake down the wall of Jerusalem, and burnt all the palaces thereof with fire, and destroyed all the goodly vessels thereof. 20 And them that had escaped from the sword carried he away to Babylon; where they were servants to him and his sons until the reign of the kingdom of Persia:

Babylon Empire Number Three, (last days) Mystery Babylon

Lastly, Babylon appears in the end times *Revelation 17, 18*. Not only does it appear thousands of years in the future after Apostle John wrote (90 AD) but God declares it a mystery. If the pattern holds true as it did for Babylon Number one and two, then Mystery Babylon's characteristics mimic her predecessors: It should be a great nation with a great city. It should seek world dominance- Be the#1 military power on earth. It should have the greatest city on earth, including a fascination for tall buildings. And be a center for God's people.

So then the spiritual attitude of Babylon spans over 4,000 years of human history. No wonder Apostle John wondered as the angel revealed to him Mystery Babylon. Babylon's whole identity remained impossible to grasp until history unfolded. From its beginning, Kingdom Babylon has been at war with the Kingdom of God, thus there is a constant spiritual element to this empire. Babylon continues to fight until she is destroyed. **Mystery Babylon is the final phase of Daniel's Fourth Kingdom**.

Revelation 17:5-6 And upon her forehead was a name written, MYSTERY, BABYLON THE GREAT, THE MOTHER OF HARLOTS AND ABOMINATIONS OF THE EARTH. 6 And I saw the woman drunken with the blood of the saints, and with the blood of the martyrs of Jesus: and when I saw her, I wondered with great admiration.

Mystery Babylon

One Kingdom manifested in two systems.

Mystery Babylon acts as the primary country ushering in a one-world government for the Antichrist. Bible students often get so involved with Revelation chapter 17; they tend to overlook the fact that two separate chapters describe Mystery Babylon. And a distinction must be made between the Babylon of Revelation chapter 17 which describes her spiritual and religious influence, and the Babylon set forth in chapter 18 which deals with her control of world commerce.

Revelation Chapter 17 -reveals the spiritual side of Babylon. False alternative religion is the spiritual, religious heart of Mystery Babylon. The present study focuses primarily on the Babylon manifested in chapter 18. Examination of chapter 17 is done only to contrast Babylon of chapter 18. The juxtaposition reveals significant differences.

Revelation chapters 17 and 18; Things that differ:

Mystery Babylon in Chapter 17 wholly concerned with spiritual matters and seducing men to hell. Like a whore, this religious harlot takes money. She does not give money, nor does she enable her customers to make money. She makes her customers feel good, and she tells them what they want to hear. The kings of the earth and all her customers are made drunk on her wine; **they are not made rich**. Her wine is primarily the false doctrine found in the cup of Roman Catholicism, but also includes additional denominations or religious bodies offering a false way to heaven. Remember the Whore is the *mother of harlots*. To limit her to one entity is incomplete and misleading.

Revelation 17:2 With whom the kings of the earth have committed fornication, and the inhabitants of the earth have been made drunk with the wine of her fornication.

The woman of chapter 17 sits on many waters. These waters scripturally defined represent the world's peoples; therefore, the woman comes to where the people live. Geographically, she prostitutes herself on every street corner on earth.

Revelation 17:1 And there came one of the seven angels which had the seven vials, and talked with me, saying unto me, Come hither; I will shew unto thee the judgment of **the great whore that sitteth upon many waters:**

Revelation 17:15 And he saith unto me, **The waters which thou sawest, where the whore sitteth, are peoples, and multitudes, and nations, and tongues.**

Now consider the Babylon of chapter 18. Here, Babylon makes the inhabitants of earth drunk,_and they are made rich. Whores do many things, but they do not make anyone rich. In chapter 18 Babylon is not called a whore. In chapter 17, God calls Babylon a whore three times.

Revelation 18:3 For all nations have drunk of the wine of the wrath of her fornication, and the kings of the earth have committed fornication with her, and the **merchants of the earth are waxed rich through the abundance of her delicacies.**

*Revelation 18:15 The merchants of these things, **which were made rich** by her, shall stand afar off for the fear of her torment, weeping and wailing,*

In chapter 18 the customers come to Babylon to sell their own wares; whereas chapter 17 Babylon goes to them to sell herself.

Revelation 18:11 And the merchants of the earth shall weep and mourn over her; for no man buyeth their merchandise any more: in **The whore operates throughout the whole earth in chapter 17, but in chapter 18 Babylon is one specific place.** The waters in 17 represent people; the waters in 18 are literal where ships bring their goods. From ocean merchant ships, grieving kings and millionaires watch their beloved city destroyed, **so last day Babylon must be a port city.** This geographic fact alone eliminates Iraq as Mystery Babylon's location.

*Revelation 18:17-19 For in one hour so great riches is come to nought. And every shipmaster, and all the company in ships, and sailors, and as many as trade by sea, stood afar off, **18** And cried when they saw the smoke of her burning, saying, What city is like unto this great city! **19** And they cast dust on their heads, and cried, weeping and wailing, saying, Alas, alas, that great city, wherein were made rich all that had ships in the sea by reason of her costliness! for in one hour is she made desolate.*

Perhaps the most striking difference between the two chapters: In 17, the kings of the earth end up hating the whore and destroying her, while in chapter 18 the kings of the earth lament and grieve over its destruction.

CONSIDER:

Revelation 17:12 And the ten horns which thou sawest are ten kings, which have received no kingdom as yet; but receive power as kings one hour with the beast.

Revelation 17:16 And the ten horns which thou sawest upon the beast, these **shall hate the whore, and shall make her desolate and naked**, *and shall eat her flesh, and burn her with fire.*

Revelation 18:8-9 Therefore shall her plagues come in one day, death, and mourning, and famine; and she shall be utterly burned with fire: for strong is the Lord God who judgeth her. 9 And the kings of the earth, who have committed fornication and lived deliciously with her, **shall bewail her, and lament for her, when they shall see the smoke of her burning,**

Observing the differences, we see Mystery Babylon manifested in two systems- **Religious and Economic.**

1. Apostate Religions whose city headquarters in Rome, and offers her cup everywhere. Notice the whore is the mother of harlots *17:5* -Many false religions owe their origin to Rome, including pagan Rome of antiquity. Think of Rome as the head Madame in charge of numerous working girls.
2. An economic commercial system, the market place for the world. A place devoted to the love of money. Rome is unquestionably the religious, spiritual head of Mystery Babylon. **But Rome is not the great commercial city displayed in Revelation 18.** Who then is this great commercial city?

Revelation 18:18 And cried when they saw the smoke of her burning, saying, What city is like unto this great city!

It's fascinating the Bible asks this very question? God expects last days' saints to answer the question. What city on earth could possibly fit the description of *Revelation chapter 18?* -Think about the vast and complex economy this city represents. Its trade and marketing status is huge.

Revelation 18:11-16 And the merchants of the earth shall weep and mourn over her; for no man buyeth their merchandise any more: 12 The merchandise of gold, and silver, and precious stones, and of pearls, and fine linen, and purple, and silk, and scarlet, and all thyine wood, and all manner vessels of ivory, and all manner vessels of most precious wood, and of brass, and iron, and marble, 13 And cinnamon, and odours, and ointments, and frankincense, and wine, and oil, and fine flour, and wheat, and beasts, and sheep, and horses, and chariots, and slaves, and souls of men. 14 And the fruits that thy soul lusted after are departed from thee, and all things which were dainty and goodly are departed from thee, and thou shalt find them no more at all. 15 The merchants of these things, which were made rich by her, shall stand afar off for the fear of her torment, weeping and wailing, 16 And saying, Alas, alas, that great city, that was clothed in fine linen, and purple, and scarlet, and decked with gold, and precious stones, and pearls!

What city enjoys the wealth and status this Babylon enjoys? Not even the wildest imagination sees Iraq as the world's market place. What city, today, is like ancient Babylon or Rome was at their zenith? The last day's Babylon is the pinnacle of international trade, diverse commerce, power, and sin. Do not forget the love of money is the root of all evil. When Antichrist rules, he controls the world's wealth! The mark of the beast is the mark of a new economic system. Satan wants more than your soul, he wants total economic control.

Revelation 13:16-17 And he causeth all, both small and great, rich and poor, free and bond, to receive a mark in their right hand, or in their foreheads: 17 And that no man might buy or sell, save he that had the mark, or the name of the beast, or the number of his name.

1 Timothy 6:10 For the love of money is the root of all evil: which while some coveted after, they have erred from the faith, and pierced themselves through with many sorrows.

Ancient Babylon and then Rome dominated the world. While Rome survives as a large city today, it hardly dominates world commerce. The world's millionaires and kings could care less if Rome were destroyed. They need a city which markets their goods.

Today, the world's financial empire towers above the world. Nowhere is the love of money more apparent than in America. Capitalism's evolution seems obsessed with loving money. And America's womb of greed births the final Babylonian metropolis, New York City. World banking is paramount in New York. So is Wall Street, the world's most important stock market. The city is the economic heart beat for America, and America is the economic heart beat for the world. The World Trade Center is in New York. So is the Community of Foreign Relations, which is nothing less than the evolved Illuminati. Most importantly, the United Nations is in New York. Already providing the skeletal framework for world government, the UN, alone, should identify New York as Babylon. When the Antichrist takes over, he will be in walking distance of the institutions running the world. He will also control the world's most powerful military, America's Army, Navy, Marines, and Air Force. If any other city on earth headquartered all these institutions, American preachers would be screaming that city was Babylon. But alas, such a beam is in our eye we cannot see the forest.

Fourth Kingdom Emerges

BABYLON –TO CONFUSE BY MIXING

BABYLON –TO CONFUSE BY MIXING

Proverbs 28:21-22 *To have respect of persons is not good: for for a piece of bread that man will transgress.* ***22*** *He that hasteth to be rich hath an evil eye, and considereth not that poverty shall come upon him.*

Since the United States began, people emigrated here from around the world. With such diverse multitudes of peoples, assimilation is a slow process. People come with their cultures, religions, languages, and customs. The country became a land of mingled peoples. America seems more like a mosaic than a melting pot. Remember what Babylon means: to confuse by mixing.

America's transformation into the final phase of Daniel's image is fueled by a steadily worsening economy. Simple math really, if a majority of people decide their best hope for success or happiness is to vote for radical reforms, even if it means changing laws and giving away personal freedoms, they will do it. The tipping point is rapidly approaching. For a multitude of reasons, more and more people become increasingly dependent on the government. Money answereth all things.

The bad economy reveals another ugly truth about Americans; we don't like each other. Ascribing blame to various groups and ideologies is overt, brutal, and common. Even though Americans love their country, Americans don't like Americans. Our bickering is endless and no doubt each group has something important to say. But when it becomes a weakness or an act of betrayal to even try and understand the other side, let alone compromise, the nation is in real trouble. If only Americans would listen to each other, maybe something would get done. But that's the rub, isn't it? We are all so opinionated and sure of ourselves; we have become a nation of acrimonious accusers of one another? Empathy is mocked as weakness. Scapegoats, always in fashion; but now we really need some.

Matthew 12:25 And Jesus knew their thoughts, and said unto them, Every kingdom divided against itself is brought to desolation; and every city or house divided against itself shall not stand:

It is folly to blame one political party or a particular group for the country's overall condition. Our situation is the result of people rejecting Jesus Christ, there is no fear of God before America's eyes. The world has no king but Caesar; and Caesar is acting like Caesar, he always has, and he always will. The only nation on this earth whose constitution was written by God is Israel. And until Israel receives Jesus Christ, even they are a moral mess.

Mark 12:17 And Jesus answering said unto them, Render to Caesar the things that are Caesar's, and to God the things that are God's. And they marvelled at him.

2 Corinthians 6:17-18 Wherefore come out from among them, and be ye separate, saith the Lord, and touch not the unclean thing; and I will receive you, 18 And will be a Father unto you, and ye shall be my sons and daughters, saith the Lord Almighty.

The End Game

§

AMERICA'S ECONOMIC COLLAPSE CHANGES EVERYTHING. Europe is bankrupt. Asia loses her market place. Desperate conditions necessitate a new world order. Nations surrender much of their sovereign status just to survive. The greatest market on earth is broke. With no one to buy the world's goods, unsold products rot on the docks. The cascading economic disaster gets worse and worse.

*Daniel 7:23-25 Thus he said, The fourth beast shall be the fourth kingdom upon earth, which shall be diverse from all kingdoms, and shall devour the whole earth, and shall tread it down, and break it in pieces. 24 And **the ten horns out of this kingdom are ten kings that shall arise:** and another shall rise after them; and he shall be diverse from the first, and he shall subdue three kings. 25 And he shall speak great words against the most High, and shall wear out the saints of the most High, and think **to change times and laws:** and they shall be given into his hand until a time and times and the dividing of time.*

*Revelation 17:12 **And the ten horns which thou sawest are ten kings**, which have received no kingdom as yet; but receive power as kings one hour with the beast.*

King Nebuchadnezzar's vision of the image's lowest point (the last days) is the feet. Feet have ten toes, a direct reference to the ten kings. The feet reveal the Fourth Kingdom in its final condition.

We see iron toes mixed with clay. These ten kings, represented by the toes, are supernatural beings. Notice they mingle themselves with the seed of men. But they look like men and have extraordinary abilities. Just as in the days of Noah, human seed is mixed with angels. The Fourth Kingdom's emergence is clearly not a smooth sailing operation. It is partly strong, partly broken; but none the less, it is governing the world. Most importantly, for the student of prophecy, the ten kings are in place before the Antichrist takes over. They could definitely be ruling before the Tribulation begins. (Jude)

Governmentally, the world divides into ten political regions. Ten governors lead these territories while remaining under the authority of the hegemonic Fourth Kingdom.

*Daniel 2:40-44 And the fourth kingdom shall be strong as iron: forasmuch as iron breaketh in pieces and subdueth all things: and as iron that breaketh all these, shall it break in pieces and bruise. 41 And whereas thou sawest the feet and toes, part of potters' clay, and part of iron, the kingdom shall be divided; but there shall be in it of the strength of the iron, forasmuch as thou sawest the iron mixed with miry clay. 42 And as the toes of the feet were part of iron, and part of clay, so the kingdom shall be partly strong, and partly broken. 43 **And whereas thou sawest iron mixed with miry clay, they shall mingle themselves with the seed of men:** but they shall not cleave one to another, even as iron is not mixed with clay.*

Daniel 2:44 -clearly indicates the final phase of the Fourth Kingdom is just before the 2nd Coming of Jesus Christ. Jesus Christ Himself smashes the world's final kingdom. And the Millennium Kingdom replaces and consumes all surviving and surrendered Gentile nations.

Daniel 2:44 And in the days of these kings shall the God of heaven set up a kingdom, which shall never be destroyed: and the kingdom shall not be left to other people, but it shall break in pieces and consume all these kingdoms, and it shall stand for ever.

With government so partisan nothing gets done; people soon desire a temporary dictator; and they get one! (Study Julius Caesar for comparison). Knowing God destroys Babylon (the most powerful influential city on earth) Antichrist moves his seat of power to Jerusalem. Quite possibly, the United Nations moves to Jerusalem years before this happens. Such a move sets up governing posture for the Antichrist, and the predicted abomination of desolation, when the Antichrist sits in the rebuilt Jerusalem temple and declares himself deity.

A brief digression here about people thinking wise economic investments save them. When 90% of the people around you are poor and desperate; those living in comfort and luxury would be in danger from mobs. The wisest investing won't do anyone any good for very long. The idea gold or precious metals pull you through a country's total economic collapse is ridiculous. All laws are about to change. As the world postures for a dictator who knows how to fix the world's economy; no ones' wealth is worth anything. What's in your safe is not the question. What's in your heart?

Revelation 13:17 And that no man might buy or sell, save he that had the mark, or the name of the beast, or the number of his name.

Daniel 7:25 And he shall speak great words against the most High, and shall wear out the saints of the most High, and think to change times and laws: and they shall be given into his hand until a time and times and the dividing of time.

Proverbs 11:28 He that trusteth in his riches shall fall: but the righteous shall flourish as a branch.

America and Babylon

§

Jeremiah 1:4-10 Then the word of the LORD came unto me, saying, **5** *Before I formed thee in the belly I knew thee; and before thou camest forth out of the womb I sanctified thee,* **and I ordained thee a prophet unto the nations.** **6** *Then said I, Ah, Lord GOD! behold, I cannot speak: for I am a child.* **7** *But the LORD said unto me, Say not, I am a child: for thou shalt go to all that I shall send thee, and whatsoever I command thee thou shalt speak.* **8** *Be not afraid of their faces: for I am with thee to deliver thee, saith the LORD.* **9** *Then the LORD put forth his hand, and touched my mouth. And the LORD said unto me, Behold, I have put my words in thy mouth.* **10 See, I have this day set thee over the nations and over the kingdoms,** *to root out, and to pull down, and to destroy, and to throw down, to build, and to plant.*

God declared Jeremiah a prophet to the nations. His message prophesied to more than Israel. Gentile nations do well to listen. *Jeremiah chapters 50 and 51-* provide sister texts to *Revelation chapter 18*; a major difference, however, is Revelation 18 focuses on the city of Babylon, and these chapters focus on the country. Remember Babylon is a city and a kingdom. Bible students should read Jeremiah 50-51 carefully.

Rightly dividing these chapters is critical to correct understanding. Bible students know scripture is subject to a threefold interpretation: 1. Scripture has historical context. 2. Scripture has spiritual context. 3. Scripture has doctrinal context.

Numerous verses in Jeremiah 50-51 Babylon doctrinally apply toward the future Mystery Babylon. If this in an accurate deduction, these chapters may well be the most disturbing Scriptures American Christians can read.

The historical context concerns judgment on Nebuchadnezzar's Babylon (in Iraq). When Jeremiah is speaking (600 BC), Babylon is the empire God used to judge backsliding Judah. Indeed Babylon had already begun taking the Jews captive. Jeremiah warns them, however, Babylon itself will soon be conquered by invading forces from the north. The Medes and the Persians conquered and replaced Babylon as the world power. This is the historical contextual meaning of the prophet's warning. However, much of the content of these chapters cannot apply to ancient Babylon, because numerous specific statements are irreconcilable with the ancient power.

Consider:

ISRAEL'S CONDITION DATES THE PROPHECY IN THE LAST DAYS

Jeremiah 50:20 In those days, and in that time, saith the LORD, the iniquity of Israel shall be sought for, and there shall be none; and the sins of Judah, and they shall not be found: for I will pardon them whom I reserve.

When is Israel's iniquity all gone? Not when it returned after 70 year of Babylonian captivity. Think of the leaders and prophets after Jeremiah: Ezra, Nehemiah, Zechariah, Haggai, Malachi, even JESUS CHRIST. All of these prophets sought and found plenty of iniquity in

Israel and Judah. **It is in the Millennium when the Jewish nation is fully washed and cleaned**. Only after they accept Jesus Christ as Messiah are they cleared and pardoned. Concerning the verse's prophetic scope, doctrinal fulfillment happens in the Millennium, not in the days of Nebuchadnezzar's Babylon. Remember Daniel declares the Millennium kingdom (which is nothing less than the 2nd Coming of Lord Jesus Christ) smashes the Fourth Kingdom into pieces. Notice also, God references a reserve; this remnant is the 1/3 of Israel not killed in the Tribulation. There is no doubt- *Jeremiah 50:20* – is fulfilled shortly before the Millennium.

Description of the conquered Babylon must be future:

Another doctrinal (or literal) conflict with the condition of Babylon after the invasion, one must consider Jeremiah's description of the destroyed empire. In other words, what did Babylon look like after it was conquered?

Jeremiah 50:3 For out of the north there cometh up a nation against her, which shall make her land desolate, and none shall dwell therein: they shall remove, they shall depart, both man and beast.

The invading Medes and Persians did come from the north, but they did not make her land desolate. In fact the invaders moved right into the palace, and Babylon kept thriving as an economic metropolis. Men and beasts did not depart, everyone stayed under new landlords. Verse after verse, in these two chapters, declares no one occupies Babylon after her judgment. It is totally destroyed! But ancient Babylon continued to have a thriving population for hundreds of years. Even today, Iraq is inhabited and the city of Babylon is actually being rebuilt. Below are verses proving God has more than ancient Babylon on his mind.

Jeremiah 50:39-40 *Therefore the wild beasts of the desert with the wild beasts of the islands shall dwell there, and the owls shall dwell therein:* **and it shall be no more inhabited for ever;** *neither shall it be dwelt in from generation to generation.* **40 As God overthrew Sodom and Gomorrah and the neighbour cities thereof, saith the LORD; so shall no man abide there, neither shall any son of man dwell therein.**

Jeremiah 51:43 *Her cities are a desolation, a dry land, and a wilderness, a land wherein no man dwelleth, neither doth any son of man pass thereby.*

Jeremiah 50:13 *Because of the wrath of the LORD it shall not be inhabited, but it shall be wholly desolate: every one that goeth by Babylon shall be astonished, and hiss at all her plagues.*

Jeremiah 50:26 *Come against her from the utmost border, open her storehouses: cast her up as heaps, and destroy her utterly: let nothing of her be left.*

God likening Babylon's remains to Sodom and Gomorrah are irreconcilable with the ancient kingdom. Indeed, trained archeologists, historians, and scientists can't even find Sodom and Gomorrah (for certain). A Bible believer must attribute this judgment to the future.

Verse 50:9 is also a problem and very curious. Primarily two nations conquered Babylon, Medes and Persians. Yet, the verse declares an *assembly of great nations* -do the deed. The word *assembly* has an ominous ring, considering the United Nations meeting in New York calls itself the General Assembly. The General Assembly decides whether to use military force against a disobedient country. Ironically, the General Assembly attacked Iraq in 1991 for their invasion of Kuwait.

Jeremiah 50:9 *For, lo, I will raise and cause to come up against Babylon an* **assembly of great nations** *from the north country: and they* *shall set themselves in array against her; from thence she shall be taken: their arrows shall be as of a mighty expert man; none shall return in vain.*

GEOGRAPHY:

Below Jeremiah describes Babylon's geography. This geographic description also conflicts with any middle-eastern location. Look at a map of Iraq. Aside from the Euphrates River, it is not a land of much water. Yet several times Jeremiah mentions an abundance of water in the region. He is not talking about a desert area. To interpret these scriptures one needs to locate a place on many waters.

Jeremiah 51:13 O thou that dwellest upon many waters, abundant in treasures, thine end is come, and the measure of thy covetousness.

Jeremiah 50:38 A drought is upon her waters; and they shall be dried up: for it is the land of graven images, and they are mad upon their idols.

DESTROYING GOD'S HERITAGE:

The assembly of nations spoiling Babylon (will be) sent by God. One reason God destroyed ancient Babylon was because they were a destroyer of God's heritage. This is extremely damning. If this is doctrinally about the Fourth Kingdom, how could America be a destroyer of God's heritage? First we need to scripturally define God's heritage.

*Jeremiah 50:10-11 And Chaldea shall be a spoil: all that spoil her shall be satisfied, saith the LORD. 11 Because ye were glad, because ye rejoiced, O ye **destroyers of mine heritage**, because ye are grown fat as the heifer at grass, and bellow as bulls;*

God identifies his heritage in three categories. Below verses identify God's heritage. In other words God literally declares three entities as his heritage: **Israel, Children, and the Bible.**

1. **Israel** *Exodus 6:8 And I will bring you in unto the land, concerning the which I did swear to give it to Abraham, to Isaac, and to Jacob; and **I will give it you for an heritage: I am the LORD.***

As of 2010, America has not tried to destroy Israel; however, America's friendship toward Israel is changing. Our relationship with Israel is not as solid as it used to be. Israel depends on the United States more than anyone else. A breach in our alliance could be disastrous. For America!

2. Children

Psalms 127:3 Lo, children are an heritage of the LORD: and the fruit of the womb is his reward.

In regards to children, abortion speaks for itself. Knowing the great majority of Americans believe abortion is an acceptable method of birth control is horrifying. Legal slaughter of unborn babies looms a moral thermometer for our times. Another moral disaster is the steadily increasing business of child pornography (and pornography in general) and sexual abuse. While most Americans abhor these activities, America's culture increasingly commits these sins. Add to this, an anti-God education program, etc. How well is America taking care of her kids?

3. The Bible

Psalms 119:111 Thy testimonies have I taken as an heritage for ever: for they are the rejoicing of my heart.

Psalms 12:6-7 The words of the LORD are pure words: as silver tried in a furnace of earth, purified seven times. 7 Thou shalt keep them, O LORD, thou shalt preserve them from this generation for ever.

Concerning God's testimonies (the Bible) the majority of America is secular. The average citizen certainly does not honor or believe the scriptures. Views on the Bible are similar to perspectives on Greek myths. Even more damning, Christian colleges, as well as the majority of Baptist, Protestant, and Catholic ministers, teach their flocks the Bible is riddled with errors. They believe the most authority we have lies in flawed Hebrew and Greek manuscripts; which ultimately means Christians must trust some professor's opinion, rather than the King James Bible. Those who say God preserved his words without error are in the extreme minority. Hundreds of English bibles exist, almost all of them published in America; a bit confusing don't you think? Remember what the name Babylon means! *To confuse by mixing.*

By the way- Iraq does not abort babies, or destroy the Holy Bible. They do hate the Jews, but they do not have the power to destroy them. If America changes her attitude toward Israel, she possesses power to do Israel great harm. America has only one more strike before being guilty of trying to destroy God's entire heritage. Time will tell.

THE FOURTH KINGDOM, HINDERMOST NATION

Jeremiah 50:12 *Your mother shall be sore confounded; she that bare you shall be ashamed: behold, **the hindermost of the nations** shall be a wilderness, a dry land, and a desert.*

Another identifying feature, the *hindermost of the nations.* What does this mean? ***Hindermost* means the *furthest away.*** If hindermost means geographic distance, than Babylon is the furthest nation away from Israel, which eliminates Iraq. Perhaps God means the last significant nation to be established on earth? America is only 225 years old, definitely the hindermost nation.

Jeremiah 50:15 *Shout against her round about: she hath given her hand: her foundations are fallen, her walls are thrown down: for it is the vengeance of the LORD: take vengeance upon her; as she hath done, do unto her.*

Since ancient Babylon's walls and foundations remained up and solid after her conquest by the Medes and Persians, I conclude these walls and foundations are not physical. Could God be speaking of moral standards and righteousness the country once possessed?

A TRAP IS SET:

Jeremiah 50:24 *I have laid a snare for thee, and thou art also taken, O Babylon, and thou wast not aware: thou art found, and also caught, because thou hast striven against the LORD.*

One could argue all nations strive against the Lord, but this Babylon seems to have a unique relationship with God. The snare God sets is something the country does not see coming. Whatever the snare, it sets the stage for a total social and governmental disruption. I believe this verse goes hand in hand with *51:45-46.*

Jeremiah 51:45-46 *My people, go ye out of the midst of her, and deliver ye every man his soul from the fierce anger of the LORD. **46** And lest your heart faint, and ye fear for the rumour that shall be heard in the land; a rumour shall both come one year, and after that in another year shall come a rumour, and violence in the land, ruler against ruler.*

Notice God addresses this passage to his people, which means believers live inside this nation. And if the pattern of the first two Babylon's' continues, then a significant portion of God's people exist inside Babylon. No doubt believers caught up in the sins of their country. Exactly like God warned Israel, God warns his people their country is going to fall. Before God springs the trap, Babylon hears a rumor, something devastating is coming. God's people believe the rumor and become fearful. God's people need to flee the sins of Babylon and serve the Lord with all their might. I do not believe God tells Americans to leave the country, rather he instructs them to flee the nation's sin. It is not a time to hide away and do nothing, serve God.

(For readers in the Church Age, *2 Tim 4:5*)

2 Timothy 4:5 *But watch thou in all things, endure afflictions, do the work of an evangelist, make full proof of thy ministry.*

(For readers in the Tribulation, Revelation 14:7-13)

Revelation 14:7-13 *Saying with a loud voice, Fear God, and give glory to him; for the hour of his judgment is come: and worship him that made heaven, and earth, and the sea, and the fountains of waters. 8 And there followed another angel, saying, Babylon is fallen, is fallen, that great city, because she made all nations drink of the wine of the wrath of her fornication. 9 And the third angel followed them, saying with a loud voice, If any man worship the beast and his image, and receive his mark in his forehead, or in his hand, 10 The same shall drink of the wine of the wrath of God, which is poured out without mixture into the cup of his indignation; and he shall be tormented with fire and brimstone in the presence of the holy angels, and in the presence of the Lamb: 11 And the smoke of their torment ascendeth up for ever and ever: and they have no rest day nor night, who worship the beast and his image, and whosoever receiveth the mark of his name. 12 Here is the patience of the saints: here are they that keep the commandments of God, and the faith of Jesus. 13 And I heard a voice from heaven saying unto me, Write, Blessed are the dead which die in the Lord from henceforth: Yea, saith the Spirit, that they may rest from their labours; and their works do follow them.*

Wherever a believer finds himself when the ruin comes, remember Jerusalem. This advice may sound a bit odd, but an inexplicable bond exists between America and Israel. Most importantly when one remembers Jerusalem, one remembers the city from where Jesus Christ rules the universe.

Psalms 122:6 *Pray for the peace of Jerusalem: they shall prosper that love thee.*

Jeremiah 51:50 *Ye that have escaped the sword, go away, stand not still: remember the LORD afar off, and let Jerusalem come into your mind.*

The final Babylonian kingdom's destruction takes place over several years. We know from Revelation 18, Mystery Babylon's final demise happens during the Tribulation. It looks like God's snare sets off a time of great trouble, perhaps the beginning of Daniel's 70th week? The ensuing chaos leaves Babylon vulnerable to invasion from the north. A land invasion comes through Canada and/or Alaska. In this day and age, sophisticated electronic warfare, computer viruses capable of disrupting banking, aviation, transportation, hospitals, electrical grids, and food delivery systems. Considering the environment of the internet and the advancement of electronic warfare, Satan's title *prince of the power of the air* -is appropriate. And, as usual, the Bible is ahead of history.

Ephesians 2:2 *Wherein in time past ye walked according to the course of this world, according to* **the prince of the power of the air, the spirit** *that now worketh in the children of disobedience:*

Jeremiah 50:26 *Come against her from the utmost border, open her storehouses: cast her up as heaps, and destroy her utterly: let nothing of her be left.*

Jeremiah 50:32 *And the most proud shall stumble and fall, and none shall raise him up: and I will kindle a fire in his cities, and it shall devour all round about him.*

The UN armies come to protect the Fourth Kingdom's assets from the social disintegration erupting after God springs His trap. Their protection, however, is wholly inadequate as foreign troops and America's own citizenry turn into looting mobs. An ever growing percentage of America's poor are joining world opinion their poverty is caused by wealthy Americans consuming all their deserved wealth. America becomes a land to spoil; and the governmental metamorphosis to the Fourth Beast is complete.

Jeremiah 50:37 A sword is upon their horses, and upon their chariots, and upon all the mingled people that are in the midst of her; and they shall become as women: a sword is upon her treasures; and they shall be robbed.

The reference to mingled people is interesting. America is a racially mixed empire. No other nation in world history included so many peoples. Socially, politically, culturally, religiously, and morally- America manifests a land confused by mixing.

End

The Approaching Day

§

Thoughts on Daniel's 70th Week

*Daniel 9:24-27 Seventy weeks are **determined upon thy people** and upon thy holy city, to finish the transgression, and to make an end of sins, and to make reconciliation for iniquity, and to bring in everlasting righteousness, and to seal up the vision and prophecy, and to anoint the most Holy. 25 Know therefore and understand, that from the going forth of the commandment to restore and to build Jerusalem unto the Messiah the Prince shall be **seven weeks, and threescore and two weeks**: the street shall be built again, and the wall, even in troublous times. 26 And after threescore and two weeks shall Messiah be cut off, but not for himself: and the people of the prince that shall come shall destroy the city and the sanctuary; and the end thereof shall be with a flood, and unto the end of the war desolations are determined. 27 **And he shall confirm the covenant with many for one week**: and in the midst of the week he shall cause the sacrifice and the oblation to cease, and for the overspreading of abominations he shall make it desolate, even until the consummation, and that determined shall be poured upon the desolate.*

An in-depth knowledge of Israel's history is not necessary to comprehend the 70 week prophecy; however, one does need to know how God is counting time. The 70 weeks determined on the Jewish people are 70 weeks of 7 year periods. In other words, God considers every 7 years one week, a total of 490 years. 69 of those weeks have come and gone. This study deals largely with only the 1 remaining week, a single 7 year period of time. Bible students refer only to this final 7 year period when they discuss Daniel's 70th Week.

When Daniel gave the prophecy, the Jews were captives in Babylon. The 70 weeks began when Cyrus commanded the Jews return to Israel and rebuild Jerusalem *Ezra 1*. God divides the 70 weeks into 3 sections, 7 weeks, 62 weeks, and a final 1 week. A total of 69 weeks had elapsed when Jesus Christ was crucified. After Jesus' crucifixion, God stopped the clock; therefore, only one of the 70 weeks remains. Daniel's 70th week is the 7 years prior to Jesus' return. The last half or 3 ½ years of this week is called the great Tribulation. Although several prophets deal with the Tribulation, the primary texts are the books of Revelation and Daniel. Many Bible students equate or consider Daniel's 70th week and the Tribulation period the same period of time; however, a more scripturally accurate division is as follows: The great Tribulation happens within Daniels's 70th week. The last 7 years of Gentile rule is indeed Daniel's 70th Week, but only the last forty-two months is Tribulation.

The big question is when does the 70th week begin? Or in other words- Is there any way a Christian can calculate or identify the beginning of the last 7 years? Let's read the passage below carefully.

Daniel 9:26-27 *And after threescore and two weeks **shall Messiah be cut off**, but not for himself: and the people of the prince that shall come shall destroy the city and the sanctuary; and the end thereof shall be with a flood, and unto the end of the war desolations are determined. **27** And he shall confirm the covenant with many for one week: and in the midst of the week he shall cause the sacrifice and the oblation to cease, and for the overspreading of abominations he shall make it desolate, even until the consummation, and that determined shall be poured upon the desolate.*

"Messiah be cut off" refers to Jesus' crucifixion; therefore, Jesus' death concludes 69 weeks. Jesus' death is not for himself; rather he dies for the sins of the whole world.

About 30 years after Jesus Christ's death and resurrection, Roman armies, under the command of General Titus, destroyed Jerusalem and burned the temple. Because Titus destroying Jerusalem fits so well with the prophecy, many Bible instructors teach the *prince* refers to Titus. But, (doctrinally or literally) how could Titus confirm a distant future covenant when he lived in 70 AD?

The *prince that shall come* is not Titus; he is the Antichrist. And he will come later, much later than Titus. Read the verse again.

And the people of the prince that shall come shall destroy the city and the sanctuary; ...

The people of the prince destroyed Jerusalem, **not the prince himself.** The coming of the prince is still future. *The people of the prince* were Roman soldiers. Although Titus was their general, he was still only one of the prince's soldiers. Throughout the ages, Satan always had an army to oppose God's people.

So then- the coming prince is Antichrist. Although the Antichrist was not present, his armies destroyed Jerusalem in 70 AD, and the Antichrist, himself, appears in the flesh sometime in the future. At that time he confirms a covenant with Israel. The covenant is some kind of peace agreement. Notice the Bible does not say the prince makes the covenant- he simply confirms it. *Possibly, making and confirming the covenant is done at the same time.* **This confirmation starts Daniel's 70th week.**

The political world constantly pressures Israel to make land concessions on the West Bank. The Palestinians, backed by the United Nations, demanding a portion of Jerusalem to serve as capital for their proposed state. Ubiquitous Middle East trouble and wars eventually evolve into a global situation. Iran is precarious. Terrorists gain better weaponry every day. One thing is sure- everyone is sick of war.

What would it take for Israel to give away land, perhaps even carve up Jerusalem? One can only speculate. What if Muslims, acknowledged Israel's right to exist and gave the Jews access to the Temple Mount? The mount presently is also sacred real-estate to Islam. It is the site of the Dome of the Rock, an Islamic masque. Something happens which enables the Jews to begin sacrificing on the temple mount. Whether the Muslims agree to this or Jews do it forcefully, only time will tell.

But it has to happen, because animal sacrifices resume under the covenant. We know this because verse 27 says Antichrist causes the sacrifices to stop. And since biblical law allows sacrifices only on the temple mount, somehow the religious Jews get access to the property.

The Jews do not need a whole temple (at first); they need an altar. Around 500 BC when Israel returned from their Babylonian captivity, they faced a similar problem. Sacrifices resumed before a temple was built. Let the reader note the first sacrifices resumed for the feast of tabernacles. I believe history repeats itself. If this is true, Ezra is the key for unlocking prophetic mysteries. The Israelis are out of Babylon and back in the land in the book of Ezra.

Ezra 3:1-6 *And when the seventh month was come, and the children of Israel were in the cities, the people gathered themselves together as one man to Jerusalem. **2** Then stood up Jeshua the son of Jozadak, and his brethren the priests, and Zerubbabel the son of Shealtiel, and his brethren, and builded the altar of the God of Israel, to offer burnt offerings thereon, as it is written in the law of Moses the man of God. **3** And they set the altar upon his bases; for fear was upon them because of the people of those countries: and they offered burnt offerings thereon unto the LORD, even burnt offerings morning and evening. **4** They kept also the feast of tabernacles, as it is written, and offered the daily burnt offerings by number, according* *to the custom, as the duty of every day required; 5 And afterward offered the continual burnt offering, both of the new moons, and of all the set feasts of the LORD that were consecrated, and of every one that willingly offered a freewill offering unto the LORD. 6 From the first day of the seventh month began they to offer burnt offerings unto the LORD.* **But the foundation of the temple of the LORD was not yet laid.**

Comparing the first time God scattered his people and then gathered them back to Israel is remarkable. Extraordinary similarities exist between then and now. The Jews just returned to Israel after devastating defeats and near annihilation. Considering these similarities, it seems almost haunting how history repeats itself.

1. Compare Nebuchadnezzar's war on Israel to the holocaust in World War Two.
2. Compare the Jews return to Israel from captivity in 500 BC to the Jews return from their 2nd Diaspora in 1948.
3. There was only one ruling gentile super power in the world. Compare Babylon and America.
4. All of Israel's neighbors were hostile. Babylon (the world's superpower) forced them to leave Israel alone. Exactly like Israel's neighbors are today, and it is America who protects them.
5. Babylon financed the Jews return in 500 BC; America's money is apparent in maintaining Israel today.

Ecclesiastes 3:15 *That which hath been is now; and that which is to be hath already been; and God requireth that which is past.*

The Bride and Daniel's 70th Week

DOES THE BIBLE TELL US when the church is taken to heaven; in other words, when does the rapture happen? Emotional and quick answers may get ovations and robust amens, but only answers proved by scripture mean anything. Let the Bible student endeavor for the truth.

In his first letter to the Thessalonians, Apostle Paul, revealed information about the Christians' last generation. *1st Thessalonians 4:13-18* is the first time Thessalonians learned about the Rapture.

1 Thessalonians 4:13-18 But I would not have you to be ignorant, brethren, concerning them which are asleep, that ye sorrow not, even as others which have no hope. 14 For if we believe that Jesus died and rose again, even so them also which sleep in Jesus will God bring with him. 15 For this we say unto you by the word of the Lord, that we which are alive and remain unto the coming of the Lord shall not prevent them which are asleep. 16 For the Lord himself shall descend from heaven with a shout, with the voice of the archangel, and with the trump of God: and the dead in Christ shall rise first: 17 Then we which are alive and remain shall be caught up together with them in the clouds, to meet the Lord in the air: and so shall we ever be with the Lord. 18 Wherefore comfort one another with these words.

As you can imagine, Christians at Thessalonica were tremendously excited to hear about the coming rapture. And just like Christians living today, they all wanted to know when it happens. Some people actually said the day had come already; some proclaimed it would not come at all. They even claimed their information came directly from the Apostles. Many Christians were genuinely mistaken about what they believed. Others simply did not know what to believe. Then, as now, some people deliberately mislead the sheep. Logically, Apostle Paul addressed this situation in his second letter to the Thessalonians.

2 Thessalonians 2:1-3 Now we beseech you, brethren, by the coming of our Lord Jesus Christ, and by our gathering together unto him, 2 That ye be not soon shaken in mind, or be troubled, neither by spirit, nor by word, nor by letter as from us, as that the day of Christ is at hand. 3 Let no man deceive you by any means: for that day shall not come, except there come a falling away first, and that man of sin be revealed, the son of perdition;

Consider the above passage carefully. What is *our gathering together unto him?*-What is the day of Christ? These are very important questions. In fact, identifying this *gathering together-* is key to several prophecies.

2 Thessalonians 2:1 Now we beseech you, brethren, by the coming of our Lord Jesus Christ, and by our gathering together unto him,

Our gathering together unto him- is the rapture. What else could it be? Do not forget, Paul's first letter to the Thessalonians mentioned the rapture for the first time. Paul's second letter is addressing their concerns with precise information.

*2 Thessalonians 2:2 That ye be not soon **shaken in mind, or be troubled**, neither by spirit, nor by word, nor by letter as from us, as that **the day of Christ i**s at hand.*

Notice the gathering is also called the day of Christ. Paul tells us significant efforts take place to confuse and mislead. He warns of people speaking words, even false apostles writing letters to confuse Christians over this very issue. (And no doubt sincere and honest misunderstandings were common as well.)

Some people suggest the day of Christ, and the gathering together are synonymous with the 2nd Coming, but that doesn't make sense. Problems with the day of Christ being synonymous with the 2nd Coming are numerous. One must distinguish The 2nd Coming from the rapture. The rapture precedes the 2nd Coming. Also consider Jesus' 2nd Advent is not an exclusive Christian event. In fact it involves Israel, the world, Antichrist, and Tribulation saints. Christians return with Jesus as part of his army

Why would the Thessalonians be anxious for the 2nd Coming when they were just told about the rapture? By the time of the 2nd Coming- Christians have already been with Christ for years! In fact Christians return with Christ. By the 2nd Coming, the church has already been judged at the Judgment Seat of Christ and has been married at the Marriage of the Lamb.

Far more likely they wanted to know when the rapture happens. For Christians- the big day is the rapture! No Christian is going to be confused over whether Jesus has returned or is about to return. Our gathering together unto him is the rapture; therefore the day of Christ is the rapture. Apostle Paul uses the term, *day of Christ*- two more times. Implicit in both passages is seeing Jesus for the first time?

Php 1:10 *That ye may approve things that are excellent; that ye may be sincere and without offence till the **day of Christ**.*

Philippians 2:16 *Holding forth the word of life; that I may rejoice **in the day of Christ**, that I have not run in vain, neither laboured in vain.*

Two signs happen before the Rapture:

Apostle Paul gives two specific events that must happen before the rapture.

1   A falling away.
2   The man of sin is revealed.

2 Thessalonians 2:3 Let no man deceive you by any means: for that day shall not come, except there come a falling away first, and that man of sin be revealed, the son of perdition;

Let no man deceive you by any means: Deceptions take place! But that day shall not come (the day of our gathering) - except there comes a falling away first, and the man of sin be revealed. Christians need to come to grips with this. Not only a falling away happens; the Antichrist is revealed too. It is incorrect to teach the rapture can happen at any second, or there is nothing on God's prophetic calendar before the rapture. One could certainly make the case that a great falling away is ongoing even now. But the Antichrist has not yet been revealed. The uncomfortable prophetic fact is the man of sin must be revealed before the day of Christ.

*2 Thessalonians 2:3-5 Let no man deceive you by any means: **for that day shall not come, except there come a falling away first, and that man of sin be revealed,** the son of perdition; 4 Who opposeth and exalteth himself above all that is called God, or that is worshipped; so that he as God sitteth in the temple of God, shewing himself that he is God. 5 Remember ye not, that, when I was yet with you, I told you these things?*

Now the big question: When is the Antichrist revealed? Observing the obvious, a man sitting in the temple who proclaims himself God is definitely a revelation of the Antichrist. It is certainly in the context and the simplest explanation. However, this particular temple scene primarily reveals the abomination of desolation warned about by Daniel and Jesus. An earlier revelation of the Antichrist is possible and even likely, and does no injustice to the text.

Mark 13:14 *But when ye shall see the abomination of desolation, spoken of by Daniel the prophet, standing where it ought not, (let him that readeth understand,) then let them that be in Judaea flee to the mountains:*

Daniel 9:26-27 *And after threescore and two weeks shall Messiah be cut off, but not for himself: and the people of the prince that shall come shall destroy the city and the sanctuary; and the end thereof shall be with a flood, and unto the end of the war desolations are determined.* **27 And he shall confirm the covenant with many for one week: and in the midst of the week he shall cause the sacrifice and the oblation to cease,** *and for the overspreading of abominations he shall make it desolate, even until the consummation, and that determined shall be poured upon the desolate*

If the Antichrist sitting in the temple is the only revelation Apostle Paul warns about, then the rapture happens in the middle of Daniel's 70th Week. And a midweek rapture sends Christian leadership into great consternation and eschatological arguments (fits about when the rapture happens). The most commonly accepted dispensational doctrine is the Church is raptured before Daniel's 70th week begins. Thank God salvation is easy, because Christians seem to argue over everything else. That said, however, the ramifications of the correct position on the rapture remain serious.

Why would the Antichrist announcing he is god while sitting in the temple indicate a mid-Tribulation rapture for the Church?

Because *Daniel 9:27* -states the satanic drama in the temple happens in the middle of the week. If the warning given by Apostle Paul and *Daniel 9:27*- are addressing the same event, then the Church is not raptured until 42 months before the 2nd Coming. This would also mean the temple has to be rebuilt before the rapture.

Pre-Tribulation rapture:

On the other hand, there could be an earlier revelation of the Antichrist, before the abomination of desolation. Certainly, the confirmation of a covenant with Israel, and the confirmation it-self- reveals to Christians the identity of the Antichrist. And that confirmation is exactly 42 months before Antichrist's blasphemous announcement in the temple. Therefore Jesus evacuates his Bride just as Daniel's 70th Week begins.

Once the Antichrist is revealed, the rapture could happen at any moment. And just like in Ezra, all the Jews need to begin sacrificing is an altar; the temple could come later. Animal sacrifices are closely linked to the confirmation of the covenant. Why? Because Antichrist stopping sacrifices marks the middle of the week.

*Daniel 9:27 **And he shall confirm the covenant with many for one week:** and in the midst of the week he shall cause the sacrifice and the oblation to cease, and for the overspreading of abominations he shall make it desolate, even until the consummation, and that determined shall be poured upon the desolate.*

We can conclude Daniel's 70th Week begins when the Antichrist confirms a covenant with Israel. If this confirmation is the revelation of Antichrist which Apostle Paul warns in *2 Thessalonians 2:3*, the rapture could happen any moment after this event. The Bride's rapture soon after the confirming of the covenant is a pre-Tribulation rapture. Notice in the middle of the week, Antichrist stops the Jewish sacrifices and initiates the *overspreading of abominations*. It looks like the agreement was kept for 3 ½ years, and then broken in the middle of the week.

Ezra 3:1-6 And when the seventh month was come, and the children of Israel were in the cities, the people gathered themselves together as one man to Jerusalem. 2 Then stood up Jeshua the son of Jozadak, and his brethren the priests, and Zerubbabel the son of Shealtiel, **and his breth-ren, and builded the altar of the God of Israel, to offer burnt of-ferings thereon, a***s it is written in the law of Moses the man of God. 3 And they set the altar upon his bases; for fear was upon them because of the people of those countries: and they offered burnt offerings thereon unto the LORD, even burnt offerings morning and evening. 4 They kept also the feast of tabernacles, as it is written, and offered the daily burnt offerings by number, according to the custom, as the duty of every day required; 5 And afterward offered the continual burnt offering, both of the new moons, and of all the set feasts of the LORD that were consecrated, and of every one that willingly offered a freewill offering unto the LORD. 6* **From the first day of the seventh month began they to offer burnt offerings unto the LORD. But the foundation of the temple of the LORD was not yet laid.**

What is the falling away?

*2 Thessalonians 2:3 Let no man deceive you by any means: for that day shall not come, **except there come a falling away first**, and that man of sin be revealed, the son of perdition;*

Answering this question is subjective, no surprise several opinions exist. Most Christians, however, agree that Christianity (in general) is spiritually and morally degenerating. The Church is permeated with false teachers, prophets, and charlatans. The love of money doth manifest! Many church leaders change the Bible to fit personal or theological ideas. Few Christians consider God's words perfect. Correcting the Bible with the Greek or Hebrew is commonplace. Equally disturbing, is the fact congregations of saved people are not the least bit bothered when they hear the Bible being corrected. This spiritual and moral declension of Christianity is the *falling away*.

2 Thessalonians 2:5-6 Remember ye not, that, when I was yet with you, I told you these things? 6 And now ye know what withholdeth that he might be revealed in his time.

And now Christians know what withholdeth. The very words of God, the prophecy itself withholds. In other words, the gathering won't happen until the prophecies just discussed occur. Apostle Paul tells Christians to calm down. Stay busy working for the Lord. Be assured, the rapture is coming.

THE MYSTERY OF INIQUITY

2 Thessalonians 2:1-17 Now we beseech you, brethren, by the coming of our Lord Jesus Christ, and by our gathering together unto him, 2 That ye be not soon shaken in mind, or be troubled, neither by spirit, nor by word, nor by letter as from us, as that the day of Christ is at hand. 3 Let no man deceive you by any means: for that day shall not come, except there come a falling away first, **and that man of sin be revealed, the son of perdition; 4 Who opposeth and exalteth himself above all that is called God, or that is worshipped; so that he as God sitteth in the temple of God, shewing himself that he is God.** *5 Remember ye not, that, when I was yet with you, I told you these things? 6 And now ye know what withholdeth that he might be revealed in his time.* **7 For the mystery of iniquity doth already work: only he who now letteth will let, until he be taken out of the way.** *8 And then shall that Wicked be revealed, whom the Lord shall consume with the spirit of his mouth, and shall destroy with the brightness of his coming:* **9** *Even him, whose coming is after the working of Satan with all power and signs and lying wonders,* **10** *And with all deceivableness of unrighteousness in them that perish; because they received not the love of the truth, that they might be saved.*

MYSTERY OF GODLINESS OPPOSES THE MYSTERY OF INIQUITY ;
1 TIM 2:16 v 2 2 THESSALONIANS 2:7

The mystery of iniquity stands opposite of the Mystery of Godliness; iniquity is a big word for sin and evil. Just as God manifests in the flesh, Satan will manifest in the flesh. The Antichrist is quite literally (biologically) the son of Satan.

God is a trinity: Father, Son (Jesus Christ), Holy Ghost
Satan is a trinity: Dragon, son (Antichrist) False Prophet

WHO IS HE?

2 Thessalonians 2:7-8 For the mystery of iniquity doth already work: **only he who now letteth will let, until he be taken out of the way. 8** *And then shall that Wicked be revealed, whom the Lord shall consume with the spirit of his mouth, and shall destroy with the brightness of his coming:*

WHO IS "HE WHO NOW LETTETH"

The pronoun "he" lacks an apparent antecedent; in other words, grammatically there is not an obvious noun to which the pronoun "he" is referring. Thus the Bible student has to infer (make an educated guess) as to who "he" is.

The passage is often interpreted as the Church or the Holy Ghost being the antecedent for the pronoun "he." The logic for this states the Holy Ghost lives in believers; therefore, when Christians are taken out the way (raptured) then the Antichrist can appear and do his work. The theory basically means the Church is stopping Satan from revealing the Antichrist. And once the Church is gone, Satan is unrestrained. For the record, the Holy Ghost being the antecedent is problematic. The real motive for this theory is to support the pre-Tribulation rapture position. But the pre-Tribulation rapture can still happen without the "he" being the Holy Ghost. This is not to argue about when the rapture happens, but one must go where the scriptural evidence leads.

Another problem is the gender. Scripture speaks about Christians collectively as female. Christians are Jesus' Bride. Scripture identifies Christians as the Lamb's wife, chaste virgin, and body in the sense of marriage to a man and woman. If this is the Church being taken out of the way, why is it not a she? It is true individual persons who receive Christ are called the sons of God John 1:12 but collectively or as a whole group, the Bride is female.

2 Corinthians 11:2　*For I am jealous over you with godly jealousy: for I have espoused you to one husband, that I may present you as a chaste virgin to Christ.*

Revelation 21:9　*And there came unto me one of the seven angels which had the seven vials full of the seven last plagues, and talked with me, saying, Come hither, I will shew thee the bride, the Lamb's wife.*

Revelation 21:2　*And I John saw the holy city, new Jerusalem, coming down from God out of heaven, prepared as a bride adorned for her husband.*

John 3:29　*He that hath the bride is the bridegroom: but the friend of the bridegroom, which standeth and heareth him, rejoiceth greatly because of the bridegroom's voice: this my joy therefore is fulfilled.*

Ephesians 5:30-33　*For we are members of his body, of his flesh, and of his bones. 31 For this cause shall a man leave his father and mother, and shall be joined unto his wife, and they two shall be one flesh. 32 This is a great mystery: but I speak concerning Christ and the church. 33 Nevertheless let every one of you in particular so love his wife even as himself; and the wife see that she reverence her husband.*

HOLY GHOST STILL HERE AFTER THE BRIDE IS RAPTURED

Another argument is the Holy Ghost remains on the earth after Christians are gone. During the Tribulation God pours out the

Holy Spirit on all flesh in an unprecedented way. There are 144,000 spirit filled, saved Jews working to turn Israel and the world to Jesus Christ (Re.7) In fact during the Tribulation millions of people turn to Christ. It is true these Tribulation saints will not be part of the Bride (Christian Church) but the Holy Ghost definitely works their salvation.

Joel 2:28-32 *And it shall come to pass afterward,* **that I will pour out my spirit upon all flesh;** *and your sons and your daughters shall prophesy, your old men shall dream dreams, your young men shall see visions: 29 And also upon the servants and upon the handmaids in those days will I pour out my spirit. 30 And I will shew wonders in the heavens and in the earth, blood, and fire, and pillars of smoke. 31 The sun shall be turned into darkness, and the moon into blood, before the great and the terrible day of the LORD come.*

Revelation 7:9-17 *After this I beheld, and, lo,* **a great multitude, which no man could number, of all nations, and kindreds, and people, and tongues, stood before the throne, and before the Lamb, clothed with white robes,** *and palms in their hands; 10 And cried with a loud voice, saying, Salvation to our God which sitteth upon the throne, and unto the Lamb. ....* **13 And one of the elders answered, saying unto me, What are these which are arrayed in white robes? and whence came they? 14 And I said unto him, Sir, thou knowest. And he said to me, These are they which came out of great tribulation,** *and have washed their robes, and made them white in the blood of the Lamb*

MICHAEL THE ARCHANGEL THEORY

Ultimately, Satan can't make any move unless God allows him. God has empowered a supernatural being to battle Satan throughout the ages, Michael the archangel. Michael seems to be Satan's constant nemesis. Michael also appears equal or perhaps greater in strength than the anointed cherub. Certainly when one considers Michael's God, Michael is stronger. When Michael steps aside, the mystery of iniquity is unrestrained. Ponder the verses below showing Michael's constant opposition to Satan.

Jude 1:9 Yet Michael the archangel, when contending with the devil he disputed about the body of Moses, durst not bring against him a railing accusation, but said, The Lord rebuke thee.

Observe it was Michael who stopped Satan from using the body of Moses. Michael stands in the way of the devil.

Daniel 12:1 And at that time shall Michael stand up, the great prince which standeth for the children of thy people: and there shall be a time of trouble, such as never was since there was a nation even to that same time: and at that time thy people shall be delivered, every one that shall be found written in the book.

Notice *Daniel 12:1* - Michael is actually in the Tribulation period. The Michael theory asserts just prior to the great Tribulation, God orders Michael to step out of Satan's way. Thus Michael the archangel is the "he" who has been letting Satan operate within controlled boundaries allowed by God.

Daniel 10:13 But the prince of the kingdom of Persia withstood me one and twenty days: but, lo, Michael, one of the chief princes, came to help me; and I remained there with the kings of Persia.

Daniel 10:21 But I will shew thee that which is noted in the scripture of truth: and there is none that holdeth with me in these things, but Michael your prince.

During Daniel's captivity in Babylon, the prophet engaged in a great spiritual battle. Daniel was the human object in a great episode of spiritual warfare. Powerful beings pitted in battle within the spirit realm. It was Michael, called a chief prince, who was summoned to help a weaker angel.

Revelation 12:7-9 *And there was war in heaven: Michael and his angels fought against the dragon; and the dragon fought and his angels,* ***8*** *And prevailed not; neither was their place found any more in heaven.* ***9*** *And the great dragon was cast out, that old serpent, called the Devil, and Satan, which deceiveth the whole world: he was cast out into the earth, and his angels were cast out with him.*

Michael the archangel literally over powers Satan and casts him to the earth during Daniel's 70th Week; therefore, scriptures place Michael directly involved with the mystery of iniquity during the Tribulation.

Counting Days

THIS CHAPTER MEANS TO CULTIVATE thought and study; especially for future believers.

Daniel 12:11-13 *And from the time that the daily sacrifice shall be taken away, and the **abomination that maketh desolate** set up, **there shall be a thousand two hundred and ninety days.** 12 Blessed is he that waiteth, **and cometh to the thousand three hundred and five and thirty days.** 13 But go thou thy way till the end be: for thou shalt rest, and stand in thy lot at the end of the days.*

To believers nervous or even opposed to counting days, why would God instruct Daniel to prophesy these numbers if no one was supposed to understand them? Someday somewhere God expects believers to do the math. For believers inside the Tribulation, this is crucial. During Daniel's 70th Week the Jews resume animal sacrifice, apparently part of the deal for getting the covenant confirmed. But Antichrist betrays the covenant and stops allowing animal sacrifices. The very day animal sacrifice stops- there are 1290 days till the second coming of Jesus Christ.

So much is happening in the last 7 years, God breaks it down to literal 24 hour days. Since Daniel is the prophet dealing with the history of Gentiles, I use a Gentile (Roman) calendar for computing dates: Since the 70th Week includes 42 months of great Tribulation, those days are also considered.

1 year = 365 days. Daniel's 70th Week has a total of 2,557 days (2 days added for leap years).

42 months = 1279 days

Therefore **when animal sacrifices stop and the abomination of desolation is set up, 1290 days remain until the 2nd Advent of Jesus Christ.**

Very important information for anyone still around during this time! The Bible does not identify the whole 70th week as great Tribulation, only 42 months. This is determined by comparing Jesus' comments with Daniels'

*Matthew 24:15-21 When ye therefore **shall see the abomination of desolation, spoken of by Daniel the prophet, stand in the holy place, (whoso readeth, let him understand:) 16** Then let them which be in Judaea flee into the mountains: 17 Let him which is on the housetop not come down to take any thing out of his house: 18 Neither let him which is in the field return back to take his clothes. 19 And woe unto them that are with child, and to them that give suck in those days! 20 But pray ye that your flight be not in the winter, neither on the sabbath day: 21 **For then shall be great tribulation,** such as was not since the beginning of the world to this time, no, nor ever shall be.*

Matthew 24:36 But of that day and hour knoweth no man, no, not the angels of heaven, but my Father only.

Matthew 24:36 doctrinally refers to the 2nd Coming, not the Rapture, although both events are closely linked. When Jesus made the above statement, no one did know. **But when Daniel's prophecy is fulfilled, everything changes.** Once the abomination of desolation erects, and the sacrifices cease- God gives the exact number of days remaining. Jews in the Tribulation will know the very week, if not the day of Jesus' 2nd Advent.

Hypothesis- Order

* Great falling away
* Antichrist confirms covenant with Israel. Daniel's 70th week begins, **2,557 days till Jesus' 2nd Advent.**
* Rapture. Christians removed from earth.
* 257 days after Daniel's 70th week begins, the Jews commence Old Testament style animal sacrifice. As in the days of Ezra, the altar sacrifices begin before the temple is built. After the first sacrifice 2,300 days remain until the 2nd Coming of Jesus Christ.
* Temple construction completes.
* Abomination of desolation. Antichrist sits in the temple and declares himself God.
* Sacrifices cease. The very day animal sacrifice stops- 1290 days remain till the second coming of Jesus Christ.
* Great Tribulation begins 11 days before the abomination of desolation.
* Great Tribulation last 1279 days.
* 1335 days after Daniel's 70th begins (56 days after the abomination) something happens. **Another scenario** is on day 922 of the 70th Week- God saves the entire nation of Israel. (2257 – 1335 = 922)
* Jesus Christ 2nd Advent

WHO IS WAITING?

Daniel 12:12 *Blessed is he that waiteth, and cometh to the thousand three hundred and five and thirty days.*

The verse inspires two questions. Who are the waiting believers inside Daniel's 70th Week? And from where do they count 1,335 days?

Remember Daniel's 70th Week totals 2,557 days. If we start counting at the beginning of the week, 1335 into the week would be 56 days past the middle, or in other words 56 days into the great Tribulation. If we start counting from the middle of the week, 1335 days would put us 56 days past the 2nd Coming.

So one logical place to start counting is the beginning of the week; therefore, whoever is waiting can expect something to happen 56 days after the abomination of desolation is set up. Perhaps the entire nation of Israel is saved.

Romans 11:25-26 *For I would not, brethren, that ye should be ignorant of this mystery, lest ye should be wise in your own conceits; that blindness in part is happened to Israel, until the fulness of the Gentiles be come in.* ***26*** *And so all Israel shall be saved: as it is written, There shall come out of Sion the Deliverer, and shall turn away ungodliness from Jacob:*

ANOTHER CURIOUS PROPHECY FROM THE BOOK OF DANIEL.

Daniel 8:9-14 *And out of one of them came forth a little horn, which waxed exceeding great, toward the south, and toward the east, and toward the pleasant land.* ***10*** *And it waxed great, even to the host of heaven; and it cast down some of the host and of the stars to the ground, and stamped upon them.* ***11*** *Yea, he magnified himself even to the prince of the host, and by him the daily sacrifice was taken away, and the place of his sanctuary was cast down.* ***12*** *And an host was given him against the daily sacrifice by reason of transgression, and it cast down the truth to the ground; and it practised, and prospered.* ***13*** *Then I heard one saint speaking, and another saint said unto that certain saint which spake, **How long shall be the vision concerning the daily sacrifice, and the transgression of desolation, to give both the sanctuary and the host to be trodden under foot?*** **14**

And he said unto me, Unto two thousand and three hundred days; then shall the sanctuary be cleansed.

What are these 2,300 days? This is inside Daniel's 70ᵗʰ Week, because the little horn is Antichrist, animal sacrifice and the sanctuary are present. But 2,300 days are 257 days short of 7 years (2,557 days).

Daniel asks a question *8:13* -how long the transgression of desolation is going to be allowed to go on, (my paraphrase) the answer is 2300 days and then the sanctuary is cleansed. Since Daniel's question concerns sacrifice, it seems logical to start counting from the day the Jews commenced animal sacrifices. But how do we know what day? By subtracting 2300 days from the total number of days in the week, we arrive at day 257 days after the confirmation of the covenant. **In other words, 257 days after Daniel's 70ᵗʰ week begins the Jews commence Old Testament style animal sacrifice.**

After the first sacrifice 2,300 days remain until the 2ⁿᵈ Coming of Jesus Christ. And the sanctuary is cleansed the day Jesus returns (and or) the day after Armageddon.

Counting in the middle of the week, 2300 days from mid-week would be 1021 days after the Jesus 2ⁿᵈ Coming.

THOUGHT TO PONDER:

How many days between *Ezra 3:6 and 3:8?* The altar stood alone (on the land) before the building of the temple commenced for a brief period of time. Do you think 257 days is the answer?

Ezra 3:6 From the first day of the seventh month began they to offer burnt offerings unto the LORD. But the foundation of the temple of the LORD was not yet laid.

Ezra 3:8 Now in the second year of their coming unto the house of God at Jerusalem, in the second month, began Zerubbabel the son of Shealtiel, and *Jeshua the son of Jozadak, and the remnant of their brethren the priests and the Levites, and all they that were come out of the captivity unto Jerusalem; and appointed the Levites, from twenty years old and upward,* **to set forward the work of the house of the LORD.**

Ezra 3:1-6 And when the seventh month was come, and the children of Israel were in the cities, the people gathered themselves together as one man to Jerusalem. 2 Then stood up Jeshua the son of Jozadak, and his brethren the priests, and Zerubbabel the son of Shealtiel, **and his brethren, and builded the altar of the God of Israel, to offer burnt offerings thereon,** *as it is written in the law of Moses the man of God. 3 And they set the altar upon his bases; for fear was upon them because of the people of those countries: and they offered burnt offerings thereon unto the LORD, even burnt offerings morning and evening. 4 They kept also the feast of tabernacles, as it is written, and offered the daily burnt offerings by number, according to the custom, as the duty of every day required; 5 And afterward offered the continual burnt offering, both of the new moons, and of all the set feasts of the LORD that were consecrated, and of every one that willingly offered a freewill offering unto the LORD. 6 **From the first day of the seventh month began they to offer burnt offerings unto the LORD. But the foundation of the temple of the LORD was not yet laid.**

End

Jesus' Warning

§

MATTHEW 24:15-21 WHEN YE THEREFORE shall see the abomination of desolation, spoken of by Daniel the prophet, stand in the holy place, (whoso readeth, let him understand:) 16 Then let them which be in Judaea flee into the mountains: 17 Let him which is on the housetop not come down to take any thing out of his house: 18 Neither let him which is in the field return back to take his clothes. 19 And woe unto them that are with child, and to them that give suck in those days! 20 But pray ye that your flight be not in the winter, neither on the sabbath day: 21 For then shall be great tribulation, such as was not since the beginning of the world to this time, no, nor ever shall be.

In *Matthew 24:15-21*, Jesus is elaborating on the middle of the week! Verse 21 is very clear. Jesus identifies the time coming after the abomination-as the great *Tribulation*. This corresponds directly with Antichrist breaking the covenant in *Dan 9:27*.

Revelation 13:2-9 And the beast which I saw was like unto a leopard, and his feet were as the feet of a bear, and his mouth as the mouth of a lion: and the dragon gave him his power, and his seat, and great authority. 3 And I saw one of his heads as it were wounded to death; and his deadly wound was healed: and all the world wondered after the beast. 4 And they worshipped the dragon which gave power unto the beast: and they worshipped the beast, saying, Who is like unto the beast? who is able to make *war with him? 5 And there was given unto him a mouth speaking great things and blasphemies; **and power was given unto him to continue forty and two months.** 6 And he opened his mouth in blasphemy against God, to blaspheme his name, and his tabernacle, and them that dwell in heaven. 7 And it was given unto him to make war with the saints, and to overcome them: and power was given him over all kindreds, and tongues, and nations. 8 And all that dwell upon the earth shall worship him, whose names are not written in the book of life of the Lamb slain from the foundation of the world. 9 If any man have an ear, let him hear.*

Revelation 13:2-9 is loaded with information. The beast is another name for Antichrist. Apparently (in verse 3) the Antichrist is killed and returns to life- No doubt some type of mock resurrection. But he continues 42 months! The Antichrist *continuing* means he was already on the earth and in power. But in his last 42 months, he reveals his true ambitions. Again this is right in the middle of Daniel's 70th week. Not implying the first 3 ½ years is a smooth ride- but it's nothing like the last 42 months.

Salvation

§

IN THE JOHN CHAPTER 3, Jesus made a disturbing statement to a man named Nicodemus:

John 3:3 Jesus answered and said unto him, Verily, verily, I say unto thee, Except a man be born again, he cannot see the kingdom of God.

Jesus' statement is disturbing because Nicodemus believed in God, and thought he was prepared to go to heaven, but Jesus says he was not ready. Nicodemus asks a logical question:

John 3:4 Nicodemus saith unto him, How can a man be born when he is old? can he enter the second time into his mother's womb, and be born?

What exactly does Jesus mean anyway? Being *born again* is synonymous with salvation, in other words, being ready to go to heaven. The most important decision a person can make is to be born again-*Except a man be born again, he cannot see the kingdom of God.*

HAVE YOU BEEN BORN AGAIN? ARE YOU ABSOLUTELY CERTAIN YOU ARE SAVED AND WILL GO TO HEAVEN WHEN YOU DIE?

Many people are like Nicodemus. They believe in God, and they believe they are good enough (at least compared to lots of other people). Besides, with so much religious confusion, and everyone thinks they're right- what else can a person possibly do other than be good as possible?

CONSIDER THIS:

Since Jesus said *you must be born again* this also means there was a time in your life when you were not born again. Do you remember a time when you were not saved?

Compare this question to asking a married couple when they got married. A married person may forget the day or the year of the wedding, but it is very unlikely anyone forgets being single. In other words, they remember when they were not married. Lots of people forget the exact date of their anniversary, but no one forgets the wedding happened.

Do you remember when you were not saved?
If you can't remember being lost, you are probably not saved.

Imagine standing before God on Judgment Day, and God asks, **What have you done to deserve heaven?** What is your answer? Below is a sampling of wrong answers:

- I believe in God
- Basically I'm a good person.
- Although I'm a sinner, I did my best.
- I am generous with my money.
- I help people whenever I can.
- I'm not that bad, compared to some.
- I go to church.
- I pray.

- I have been baptized.
- I have been confirmed.

These answers are all wrong because they imply a person must earn heaven by good works. Most people believe they go to heaven because they are good enough. They conclude a loving God lets them in to heaven because they are basically OK. But this conclusion also rejects one's personal need for a Saviour.

- What do you believe?
- Are you counting on good works or Jesus?
- Do you want to get just what you deserve?

Personal moral goodness does not earn salvation. One can be religiously and morally good and still reject Jesus Christ. Actually, this is the difference between Christianity and all other religions. After all is said and done, every other religion (including secular humanism) teaches the way people behave (moral conduct) earns their eternal reward. While Christianity teaches the only way to heaven is by making Jesus Christ your personal Saviour. Through faith, God covers your sin with His blood, and gives you the righteousness of Jesus Christ. Salvation is a gift; accepting that gift by faith is the only thing a person can do.

The verses below reveal God's conclusion on the moral goodness of mankind. As you can see, any bragging about personal goodness is pride and foolishness.

Romans 3:10-18 As it is written, There is none righteous, no, not one: 11 There is none that understandeth, there is none that seeketh after God. 12 They are all gone out of the way, they are together become unprofitable; there is none that doeth good, no, not one. 13 Their throat is an open sepulchre; with their tongues they have used deceit; the poison of asps is under their lips: 14 Whose mouth is full of cursing and bitterness: 15 Their feet are swift to shed blood: 16 Destruction and misery are in their ways: 17 And the way of peace have they not known: 18 There is no fear of God before their eyes.

According to God's Word, we are all sinners and in need of repentance. Don't deceive yourself because so many people are worse than you. Repentance means being willing to change or turn from old attitudes, and ideas about God, just as much as it means being willing to change behavior. It may be your life style isn't all that bad, but have you been saved?

Going to church, giving money to worthy causes, and moral goodness is commendable, but beware; you can be a good person and still be lost. When it comes to getting into heaven, the only righteousness God accepts is the righteousness of Jesus Christ. And the only way to get Christ's righteousness is to believe in Him and ask Jesus to save you. When a person makes Jesus his/her Saviour, Jesus imputes or gives His righteousness to them.

Romans 3:21-25 *But now the righteousness of God without the law is manifested, being witnessed by the law and the prophets; 22 Even the righteousness of God which is by faith of Jesus Christ unto all and upon all them that believe: for there is no difference: 23 For all have sinned, and come short of the glory of God; 24 Being justified freely by his grace through the redemption that is in Christ Jesus: 25 Whom God hath set forth to be a propitiation through faith in his blood, to declare his righteousness for the remission of sins that are past, through the forbearance of God;*

Ephesians 2:8-9 *For by grace are ye saved through faith; and that not of yourselves: it is the gift of God: 9 Not of works, lest any man should boast.*

John 3:16 *For God so loved the world, that he gave his only begotten Son, that whosoever believeth in him should not perish, but have everlasting life.*

Romans 10:9-10 That if thou shalt confess with thy mouth the Lord Jesus, and shalt believe in thine heart that God hath raised him from the dead, thou shalt be saved. 10 For with the heart man believeth unto righteousness; and with the mouth confession is made unto salvation.

Romans 10:13 For whosoever shall call upon the name of the Lord shall be saved.

In our natural condition we are separated from God by our sin. The whole world is a morally fallen mess. No one is born righteous, good, or in love with God. There comes a time in your life when you must make a choice. And the choice is to get saved or to stay lost.

Have you ever acknowledged your own lost condition and your need of salvation? A person can actually believe the Bible and still be trusting in his/her own good works. A lot of church going folks never call on the Lord for their own personal salvation. Do you remember a time in your life when you prayed for the Lord Jesus Christ to save you? If your answer is no, or you are not sure, read the verses below and do it now.

Romans 10:13 For whosoever shall call upon the name of the Lord shall be saved.

There is no other way. No other religion. No other God. Jesus, alone, is the Saviour of your soul. Salvation is in Christ alone. Without Jesus Christ as your Saviour you are lost. The Bible is very plain.

John 14:6 Jesus saith unto him, I am the way, the truth, and the life: no man cometh unto the Father, but by me.

John 14:9 Jesus saith unto him, Have I been so long time with you, and yet hast thou not known me, Philip? he that hath seen me hath seen the Father; and how sayest thou then, Shew us the Father?

1 John 5:12-13 He that hath the Son hath life; and he that hath not the Son of God hath not life. 13 These things have I written unto you that believe on the name of the Son of God; that ye may know that ye have eternal life, and that ye may believe on the name of the Son of God.

John 3:15-17   That whosoever believeth in him should not perish, but have eternal life. 16 For God so loved the world, that he gave his only begotten Son, that whosoever believeth in him should not perish, but have everlasting life. 17 For God sent not his Son into the world to condemn the world; but that the world through him might be saved.

Romans 10:9-13 That if thou shalt confess with thy mouth the Lord Jesus, and shalt believe in thine heart that God hath raised him from the dead, thou shalt be saved. *10* For with the heart man believeth unto righteousness; and with the mouth confession is made unto salvation. *11* For the scripture saith, Whosoever believeth on him shall not be ashamed. *12* For there is no difference between the Jew and the Greek: for the same Lord over all is rich unto all that call upon him. *13* For whosoever shall call upon the name of the Lord shall be saved.

End

About the Author

CHAPLAIN JOSEPH DULMAGE EARNED HIS bachelor of science degree in secondary education from Eastern Michigan University with a focus on history, psychology, and social studies.

Dulmage worked as a chaplain in the Life Connections Program in federal prisons, serving Christ in the forbidding environments of USP Leavenworth and USP Terre Haute. He also worked as the director of prisoner aftercare with Volunteers of America's national office and as the facilitator of LCP in Michigan's FCI Milan prison.

Dulmage's career includes experience as a public school teacher, Bible teacher, counselor, and freelance writer. He is a contributing writer for Truthought Corrective Thinking, LLC.

Abraham's bosom: a place inside this earth where saved souls resided before the death and resurrection of Jesus Chirst. Also called paradise.

Adoption: Bible word for the Rapture. Compare Ro 8:23, Ephes 1:5, with1 Cor 15:52-53.

Anak: A giant.

Anakims: A giant tribe.

Angel: A supernatural being, not human but called a man.

Antecedent: In grammar, an **antecedent** is a noun, noun phrase, or clause to which a pronoun or anaphor refers.

Antediluvian: Era in history beginning with Adam and lasting till Noah's Flood.

Antediluvian: Noah's world before the flood

Antichrist: Also called man of sin, son of perdition, the Beast. He rules the world for a brief time during the Tribulation.

Arba: Father of Anak. The word Arba *means one of the four*.

Beast: another title of the Antichrist

Daniel's 70ᵗʰ Week: the final 7 years on earth preceding the 2ⁿᵈ Coming of Jesus Christ.

Deep: Astronomically huge body of water separating the 2ⁿᵈ and 3ʳᵈ heaven.

Eschatology: study of end times especially related to biblical ideas.

Etymology: The study of the origin and history of words.

False Prophet: a supernatural religious being who rules with Antichrist during the Tribulation. He directs mankind to worship the Beast. Part of the satanic trinity. Revelation 13; 16:13

Firmament: As defined by Genesis 1:8, it is Heaven, outer space, universe, space containing the 1ˢᵗ and 2ⁿᵈ heavens.

Fourth Beast: final phase description of the Fourth Kingdom. *Daniel 7:23-25*

Fourth Kingdom: last of the great gentile empires depicted in King Nebuchadnezzar's dream, interpreted by the prophet Daniel. *Daniel 2:40*

Gap fact: The theological term for the doctrine teaching an indeterminate amount of time between Genesis 1:1 and Genesis 1:2

Gap theory: The theological term for the idea there is an indeterminate amount of time between Genesis 1:1 and Genesis 1:2

Garden of Eden: Garden paradise where Adam and Eve lived before the Fall.

Giant: Offspring of an angel and a human woman.

Goliath: A small giant 9'6" tall. An enemy of Israel

Hegemony: One political entity or state leading other states, predominant influence, or domination, esp. as exercised by one nation over others.

Jeremiah: Old Testament Prophet declared a prophet to the nations. *Jeremiah 1:4-10*

Jerusalem: Capital of Israel. Capital of the Kingdom of Heaven (universe). City where God put his Throne. **Ezek 43:7**

Mid-Tribulation rapture theory: The church is raptured in the middle of Daniel's 70th week.

Millennium: one thousand year dispensation commencing with the 2nd Coming. Revelation 20

Mystery Babylon: Last days' financial capital city of the Fourth Kingdom; also the spiritual entity of alternative religions opposing God for thousands of years.

Nazarene: A person from Nazareth.

Nazareth: A city in Israel.

Nazarite: A person who makes a distinct, religious vow, incorporating a particular set of behaviors. Numbers 6

Noah's flood: A flood that covered the entire earth.

Og: A giant. 12-13 feet tall.

Paradise: Place where saved souls went after death. Located inside the earth. Also called Abraham's bosom.

Post-Tribulation theory: The church remains on earth until the 2nd Coming of Jesus. In other words- the Church goes through the whole Daniel's 70th Week, including the great Tribulation period. In this interpretation, there is still a rapture; but it happens the same day as the 2nd Coming.

Preadamite: An age or world existing before the creation of Adam.

Pre-Tribulation rapture theory: position teaches Christians (the Church) are taken away before Daniel's 70th Week begins. Basically, this means the rapture happens at least 7 years before the 2nd Coming of Jesus Christ. This theory equates the whole Tribulation with Daniel's 70th week.

Rapture: The last generation of Christians is taken to heaven without physically dying. 1st Thessalonians 4:16,17, 1 Corinthians 15:50-54.

Regeneration: Biblical term the Millennium. (Mt. 19:28)

Satanic Trinity: The Dragon (devil), Antichrist, and False Prophet: Rev 13; 20:10

Sons of God: Angels

Tribulation: Seven years prior to the 2ⁿᵈ Coming of Jesus Christ is a time of great trouble on the earth; the Bible calls this Daniel's 70ᵗʰ Week. Many Christians believe Daniel's 70ᵗʰ week and the Tribulation period are synonymous. The final 42 months of this period is the great Tribulation. During the Tribulation, the Antichrist is ruling or trying to control the entire world.

Universal flood: Flood that filled the entire universe. Genesis 1:2 during the Gap.

Books by Joseph Dulmage
Angels, Giants, and Things under the Earth
Approaching Adventure; Understanding Heaven
Distress of Souls; Yet Trouble Came
Divorce and Remarriage for Christians
Healing
Leviathan's Nightmare; Behold the Lamb
Serious and Unusual Christian Fiction
Tongues

Made in the USA
Middletown, DE
02 November 2023

41814077R00148